Liberty, Equality, Consensus and All That Jazz at the Del Rio Bar

D1569511

Liberty, Equality, Consensus and All That Jazz at the Del Rio Bar

ERNIE HARBURG

with a "little help from our friends" Eve Silberman and Larry Behnke

ISBN-13: 9781979175135
ISBN-10: 1979175136

Every revolution needs a good bar. In Ann Arbor, Michigan that bar was the Del Rio.

In the late 1960s and early 1970s, Ann Arbor morphed from a quiet Republican university town to an epicenter of the "counterculture" and liberal-left politics. And the new Del Rio Bar became the hangout for the newly Democratic City Council members; the anti-Vietnam-War activists, including the vocal Women's Strike for Peace, and the SDS; black power activists, gays and lesbians, women's libbers—a whole range of uppity youth—to strategize, booze and enjoy great jazz.

In Liberty, Equality, Consensus and All That Jazz, social scientist/epidemiologist and former Del Rio owner Ernie Harburg shares the "warts and all" story of the social experiment that was this business establishment—somehow, miraculously run by consensus, right down to hiring and firing. The lesbian cooks who balked at hiring a male … the employee who slammed the door on would-be customers because they wore suits … Torry Harburg, co-owner, who begged haughty employees for a raise … Interwoven are an employee's memories of coming of age in the raucous, sexually promiscuous, often drugged-out but surprisingly supportive Del family. And amazingly, the Bar stayed open, sometimes just barely, until 2004.

In one quixotic bar is the story of a generation.

1973

Ernie Harburg is a social psychologist. He is a Senior Research Scientist Emeritus in Psychology and Epidemiology at the University of Michigan, author of over eighty-five research articles and President Emeritus of the Yip Harburg Foundation, which promotes both the creative works of the famous lyricist and Yip's commitment to social justice and world peace.

He is the author, with Harold Meyerson, of Who Put the Rainbow in the Wizard of Oz? Yip Harburg, Lyricist (University of Michigan Press, 1993) and, with Bernard Rosenberg, The Broadway Musical: Collaboration in Commerce and Art (New York University Press, 1993).

From 1969-2004 Harburg was a co-owner of the Del Rio Bar in Ann Arbor, Michigan.

Ernie Harburg lives in New York City with his wife Deena and their son Ben.

Brief Preface

ABOUT THIS BOOK

No one lives alone or works alone. The inspiration for this book came from many people (here nameless) who wanted the Del Rio to be on the record—especially Deena Harburg and Betty Vary. The writing was started by Eve Silberman, profile reporter for the Ann Arbor Observer. She interviewed dozens of Del Rio workers, past and present. Her initial draft was doubled by Ernie adding much material from Larry Behnke's unpublished manuscript derived from diary recordings at the time he worked at the Del Rio Bar. Larry's words are signified by indented paragraphs throughout the book. Ernie than again added to the manuscript with observations of his own and further expanded this book. He assumes final responsibility for any error or poor writing or the effects of different authors or the non-linear time frame, etc.! This is not a memoir; call it "reportage." It is told in the third person observer, warts and all. Nick Markovich actually did all the typing and assembly, and knowing where to stop; Therese Malhame did initial editing and added encouragement; finally, Steve and Shira Klein did the publishing—no easy task.

This is the story of a pioneer attempt to devise and create a democratic workplace in a local barroom.

Have fun reading!

Remember, All Stories Are True!

Ernie Harburg

To all the Del Rio Bar women:

To Victoria Jane Pedersen Harburg (Torry, first mate),
> In the midst of winter,
> we learned
> that there was in you
> an invincible summer.
> > —after Albert Camus[1]

To Elizabeth K. Vary (Betty, den mother/bookkeeper),
> All we need is love
> love, love, love, love.
> > —after John Lennon and Paul McCartney[2]

To all the other women of the Bar (the leading edge),
> And the dreams
> that you dare to dream
> really do come true.
> > —Yip Harburg ("Over the Rainbow")[3]

To Deena Ruth Zahava Rosenberg Harburg (second mate),
> You are all of the above.

—Ernie Harburg

From the fathers in my life:

If you don't love living
You are slightly uncouth
Ain't it the dignified truth?
—*Yip Harburg (my father)*[4]

What was, was
What is, is
What will be—no one knows.
—*Phillip Chessin (my first surrogate father)*

Each year I learn something new—and it costs me more.
—*Harry Pedersen (my sainted first father-in-law)*

Coito [sic] ergo sum.
—*Bernard Rosenberg (my erudite second father-in-law)*[5]

—*Ernie Harburg*

"AIN'T IT THE TRUTH?"

Life is short, short, brother!
Ain' it de truth?
An' dere is no other,
Ain' it de truth?
You gotta grab dat rainbow
While you still got your youth,
Oh! Ain' it de solid truth?

Long as there's wine and gin
To drown your troubles in,
What's all dis talk o' sin?
Rise 'n' shine and fall in line,
Get dat new religion,
Ain' it de truth?
Fo' you is dead pigeon,
Ain' it de truth?
'Cause when you're laid horizontal
In dat telephone booth,
Dere'll be no breathin' spell,
Dat's only natur-el,
Ain' it the gossipel truth?

Life is short, short, brother,
Ain' it de truth?
An' dere is no other,
Ain' it de truth?
So if you don't love livin'
You is slightly uncouth,
Oh, ain' it de dignified truth?

It's de truth, de truth
It's de solid, mellow truth.[6]

—Yip Harburg

The path to happiness is through freedom
And the path to freedom is through courage.
—*Thucydides*[7]

God forbid we should ever be twenty
years without such a rebellion.
—*Thomas Jefferson*[8]

The world is my country.
Humanity is my brothers and sisters.
To do good is my religion.
—*Thomas Paine*[9]

Where worlds are laid on, an underlife develops.
—*Erving Goffman*[10]

And that government of the people, by the people
and for the people shall not perish from the earth.
—*Abraham Lincoln*[11]

To those who cling to power through corruption
and deceit and the silencing of dissent, know
that you are on the wrong side of history.
—*Barack Obama*[12]

Preamble

We the people of the Del Rio Bar, owners, staff, and customers of Ann Arbor, Michigan, in order to create a democratic workplace, managed by consensus, secure equal justice to all, provide service, generate a fair profit, enable the pursuit of happiness, promote the arts and a good society, do ordain and establish this collective in the year of 1969.

——Ernie Harburg

Introduction

Bursting onto the scene in 1970, the Del Rio Bar in Ann Arbor, Michigan, was undeniably a creature of the social upheaval of the fifties and sixties in America. Yet, it was also shaped by the Beat Generation of the fifties and the slowly dawning changes in the city of Ann Arbor itself in the sixties and seventies as it reacted and joined the *national countercultural movements* for civil rights, antiwar dissent, full women's rights (including sexual rights for all), and protest against an ancient, authoritarian style across society's institutions.

Jazz player and Del co-owner Rick Burgess was strongly influenced by the Beat Generation, but in contrast to the more flamboyant and politically outspoken hippies of the sixties, he tended to be quietly creative, more subdued in dress and demeanor. Co-owners Ernie and Torry Harburg were also influenced by the late-fifties value challenges to the straight culture, led by Lenny Bruce,[13] Kenneth Rexroth,[14] and Jack Kerouac.[15] In the Del's early years, many of its most loyal customers were people who, in their youth, had also identified with the early movement—an underground resistance to the stifling fifties culture of Ozzie Nelson's family, Norman Rockwell's "good family people," Guy Lombardo, the return of the 1920 Republicans and their witch-hunting House Un-American Activities Committee with Joe McCarthy,[16] and, equally oppressive, the Organization Man.[17] As the poet said,

1

The flannel suit,
The Dacron smile,
The drip-dry zest that sweeps him.

You can always tell
A man these days
By the Company that keeps him.[18]

All the co-owners of the new Del Rio Bar were caught up in the major purpose of the *counterculture* of the sixties: make love, not war. Pursue life, liberty and happiness—now. *Create more democratic governance everywhere—now.*

Republicans, mostly conservative professionals, businessmen, and a few rich families had literally controlled Ann Arbor's politics for decades. The last Democratic mayor was in 1931! But in the late fifties, a glitch appeared in the Republican armor. In 1957, University of Michigan political science professor Sam Eldersveld ran, as a Democrat, for mayor. No one was more surprised than he when he won. Anticipating a defeat, he had planned to go on leave in Palo Alto, California, after the election. He had to cancel the leave. Republicans recaptured the mayoral seat in 1959 and remained the majority party for several years afterward, but Eldersveld's election was an indication that the times they were "a-changin.'"[19] For example, Ann Arbor was a "dry town" until in the late fifties–early sixties three referenda opened up the zones of "drinking by the glass"—even on campus! The first (and only) African-American mayor, Albert Wheeler, was elected in 1975. Blacks, whose first families came on the Underground Railroad in the early 1800s, were 10 percent of the population of this white, professional city. By the time the Del Rio Bar closed in 2004, the Democrats controlled city politics, while the Republicans fought for life in the new Ann Arbor, which had been a small, divided "town-and-gown" city of 100,000 dominated by the University of Michigan until the sixties and seventies, when the "downtown" area now became a stronger part of a new integrated city life.

Children during the fifties, the "baby boomers," had been exposed to the burgeoning civil rights movement of the fifties, sixties, and seventies, which included seminal events such as the 1954 *Brown v. Board of Education* decision, declaring that separate schools were not equal, Rosa Parks's refusal to give up her seat on a segregated bus, and Eisenhower's decision to send federal troops to Little Rock, Arkansas, to support school deseg-regation. Globally, the liberation of India from colonial rule by Gandhi in 1945 rolled across Africa[20] into America.[21] Here, Martin Luther King, President Lyndon Johnson,[22] the NAACP, Malcolm X, and black uprisings (labeled "riots" by the media) in 22+ cities across the nation all helped to ignite and lead a civil rights revolution.[23] Sending federal troops to quell white supremacists in southern states (Eisenhower, Kennedy, Johnson) finally ended the legal basis of racism in state laws. In the sixties, across the country, and particularly in college towns like Ann Arbor, thousands of young people grew their hair long, smoked pot, and actively protested racism in America. In 1967, the United States Supreme Court ruled that denial of interethnic/racial marriage by states was unconstitutional. The dismantling of legal grounds for a post-slavery Jim Crow society since 1865 was being initiated at last in America![24]

The counterculture generation also dissented on the Vietnam War. The waging of the war, with its mounting death toll—60,000 Americans eventually died—and implicit threat of the draft, increased their alien-ation from American society, as did the *assassinations* of civil rights leaders Medgar Evers (1963), Jack Kennedy (1963), Malcolm X (1965), Martin Luther King (1968), and Bobby Kennedy (1968). Dissent against racism and the Vietnam war was made dangerous by white supremacists allied with superpatriots. By the late sixties, the civil rights revolution had exploded in violence across the nation's cities. After the black-inspired Detroit Rebellion, a majority of Detroit and Ann Arbor citizens were against the Vietnam War—a false war with no exit plan, no victory point, and no sound purpose.[25] In 1970, four Kent State students were killed by the Ohio National Guard and students were also killed by Guards in Mississippi and elsewhere. An ever-increasing number of Americans repeatedly took to the streets to protest the Vietnam War. The establishment (then and today during the Iraq War II) ignored the petitions for the redress of grievances by the people. Government and authority were derided; the word was out not to trust anyone "over thirty."

The third large deep countercultural movement was the women's rights revolution, which exploded throughout the nation largely in the late sixties and seventies from its historical roots far back in the 1800s. Indeed, de Tocqueville predicted in the 1830s that *the idea of equality* was so radical and embedded in American culture that blacks and women would drive the cultural turmoil in the future America.[26] The new Del Rio Bar was largely made up of women who were part of this new, historically irreversible wave of legal change and enforcement of women's rights in America (including human sexual rights). In 1947–48, first-year enrollments for women in American Law schools was 3.3 percent of total enrollment; in 1970, it was 8.6 percent; and in 2005–6, it was 47.5 percent.[27] The rise in women's admissions to medical school was just as dramatic. Ann Arbor's women of all ages joined the women's rights movement. In the early seventies (unknown to most voters until after the election), a gay man and a lesbian were elected to the City Council in Ann Arbor. In 1973 the U.S. Supreme Court ruled in *Roe v Wade* that abortion was a decision for the physician and the pregnant woman.[28] In 1991 Ann Arbor elected its first woman mayor who was replaced by another woman who left office in 2000. Today, in 2007, the University of Michigan has its first woman president and also a woman full professor in the Law School who helped break national legal barriers and assert women's rights.[29] The seventies began the long journey toward legal dismantling of legal sexism in America. *Changing gender and racist attitudes in organizational culture will take a longer time!*

The fourth, less studied movement, was the counterculture challenge to authoritarian style and outdated institutional rules, for example, at universities and corporations, where dress codes and "curfew" rules were relaxed, while less rigid status behavior and more *open dissent* prevailed across the nation. "Whistleblowers" like John Dean, in the Watergate impeachment of Nixon, and Daniel Ellsberg, who exposed the Viet Nam War government falsehoods[30], are still free citizens today and legally protected. In Ann Arbor, Harburg had helped initiate a teaching research program at the University of Michigan Graduate School of Nursing and noticed that not only was "curfew" for undergrad nurses curtailed in the sixties but nationwide "strikes" were even carried out by nurses, the traditional suppressed wives. The California Nurses Association in 2008 led a large protest movement against the broken health system in favor of a national health for all concept.[31] In the sixties for the first time nurses could be trained as "clinical practitioners" in charge of wellness clinics. The old rules of an authoritarian society were being challenged throughout America by these countercultural surges.

Around the late sixties Ernie Harburg, his wife Torry Pedersen Harburg, and Harburg's friend Rick Burgess decided to open a bar in a run-down section of downtown Ann Arbor. Although well "over thirty," they all were keenly in tune with the mood of the country. Their timing proved impeccable. The Del Rio Bar became a popular gathering place for "radicals" young and old, and for all who believed in an "open" and less authoritative society and acted to make their visions become real. Until its closing day, thirty-four years later, the Del Rio continued to influence and reflect the spirit of that counterculture movement in American history and provide an experiment in democratic process.

A New Kind of Bar for Ann Arbor

In a lot of ways, it was like an old-fashioned barn-raising.

Soon after midnight one Saturday morning in November 1969, U-M research scientist Ernie Harburg, women's peace activist Torry Pedersen Harburg, and jazz musician Rick Burgess and about twenty-five of their friends met for a bite at a downtown diner. After consuming large platters of bacon and scrambled eggs, the group headed a few blocks over to the corner of Washington and Ashley. There stood the Del Rio Bar and restaurant—recently purchased by the Harburgs and Burgess.

The three owners were determined to change the tough atmosphere of the sex- and race-segregated workingman's bar. A dramatic makeover, they thought, was a good start. "We ripped the place apart," Harburg recalled.

The building's unwanted features included what he described as a "dirty, grungy orange wall" and a dropped ceiling through which they could glimpse the original tin. The raucous, friendly group began hacking away, and, to the music of the Beatles, Jimi Hendrix, the Rolling Stones, and a slight touch of Beethoven, the grungy orange plaster fell off and the handsome brick wall of the three-story 1869 building was exposed. And when former owner Phil Gentile pulled the fake ceiling down, the black pressed tin ceiling, with intricate patterns, came into its glory.

Arriving late to the "barn-raising," Julie Detwiler, employed at the Del from 1969 to 1975, found "the whole room full of plaster dust." Nonetheless, she had stepped into a scene of happy pandemonium. People were laughing and slapping each other on the back. The Harburgs' three teenage sons, supervised by Rick, stained the new wood wall paneling behind the actual bar. Determined to open as usual that evening, the unpaid volunteers worked through the day. When the 8 p.m. opening hour came, they put candles in wine bottles on the tables and triumphantly toasted the Bar's new look.

The new Del Rio was open for counterculture bar business.

Birthed in the mood of rebellion that defined Ann Arbor in the late sixties and early seventies, the Bar outlasted that turbulent era to emerge as a cherished "townie" bar, its idiosyncratic personality a marked contrast to the chain-owned drinking establishments that sprang up in later years. A promoter of music and the fine arts, the Del Rio was also influential in the rehabilitation of a once despondent downtown Ann Arbor. Although some Students for a Democratic Society (SDS) (and later the Weathermen[32]) went there, most of its hard-core patrons were longtime Ann Arborites. In its early years, regulars included members of Torry Harburg's group, Women Strike for Peace[33], not-yet-outed lesbians and gays, radicals from the thirties, self-described "hippies," just-turned-thirty beatniks, and even members of the City Council. Torry herself was the daughter of Harry Pedersen, an old-time labor activist, a Eugene Debs/Norman Thomas socialist, and president of the National Glaziers Union, who once ignored a Mafia threat on his life to speak at a labor rally. (Fortunately, the threat was never carried out.) Former city council member Larry Hunter, who was a Del Rio regular for three decades, chose to skip his law school graduation ceremony and celebrate instead at the Bar, "because they were my family."

But regulars like Hunter knew that, along with its other roles, the Del Rio was for three decades a bold workplace experiment. Until shortly before it closed for good, in the wee hours of January 1, 2004, the Bar was run collectively, with ad hoc committees that managed salaries, menus, hirings, and firings. Old-time customers grew to enjoy the look of surprise that crossed the occasional irate customer's face when he or she demanded to see the manager. "There is no manager," was the reply. That the Bar was successfully run as a collective for three decades after its opening, reflected former employee Gail Grigsby (1975–85), is "a mystery of Ann Arbor life."

In the late sixties, Ernie Harburg decided he needed a backup income. Then in his mid-forties, he had a Ph.D. in social psychology, a new and optimistic hybrid discipline that had arisen at the end of World War II. Harburg also had degrees in history and cultural anthropology. As a research scientist (still active in 2008) at the University of Michigan he conducted a major study in Detroit in the sixties on blacks and whites, their lives and their blood pressures.[34] In fact, the 12th Street area where the Detroit Rebellion started in 1967 was a focus of the research started in 1965.[35] Back in Ann Arbor on one occasion after the police cleared the riotous streets, about twenty-three students were arrested and Harburg was amused to learn that three of those arrested worked for him!

The pioneers of social psychology tended to be idealists—people who, as Harburg's onetime supervisor Bob Kahn put it, were moved by "the prospect of shaping the world into a more benign place." Reluctant to become a traditional full-time professor, Harburg essentially supported himself through "soft money"—unsolicited grants, usually from the federal government. But in the late sixties, the grant game became increasingly competitive with the Pentagon. In a move extremely unusual for an academic—especially one with a non-working wife and three children—the Harburgs decided to supplement the family income by opening a bar. Little did he and Torry know they were creating a unique experience in democracy in the workplace.

The decision wasn't just the couple's. At the University of Michigan's Institute for Social Research (ISR), the organization under whose aegis Burgess and Harburg first learned their research, Harburg had become friendly with Rick Burgess, who headed a fledgling computer department.

Larry Behnke, who wrote an affectionate memoir of the Del Rio Bar[36] from his viewpoint as a "hippie" waiter from 1972 to 1985, wrote:

Rick was ready to try something new too. He was the ultimate beatnik and his life revolved around music. He played jazz piano. He wore black Levis, black shoes, black turtlenecks, and a goatee. His thin hair was long and he sat shyly at the keyboards letting his fingers do the talking. He wanted badly to get out of data programming. Rick dreamed of opening his own place where people could hear jazz, a cool place where he could play his music.

Rick wanted a place to play where the owner wouldn't say, "Play 'Happy Birthday.'"

Born and raised in Chicago, he was exposed to a lot of fine music. In the early sixties he was playing gigs in Europe. Uncle Sam didn't care for Rick's quest and ordered him back to the states for the draft. He got out of that by enrolling at the University of Michigan, where he earned a degree in electrical engineering.

Rick got a day job at ISR where he was head of a data programming unit. Nights he joined with bassist Ron Brooks to play in Ann Arbor's first jazz combo. A mutual friend, Jack Erfurt, introduced Rick to Ernie and Torry. The three hit it off and seemed to balance each other: Rick's quiet cool, Ernie's ebullient confidence, and Torry's strong sense of justice. They made good partners because they all absolutely trusted each other.

Ann Arbor had just got its first-ever jazz hangout—the Falcon—where Rick played in the early sixties.

The trio took in a Bar manager, Ken Ishizu, who had managed two different Ann Arbor bars—one a new hippie bar called Mr. Flood's Party. After checking out several other businesses, they got in touch with Phil Gentile, owner of the Del Rio Bar. Gentile was eager to make a deal. Twice before he had sold the place only to have his buyers default on their loans. Gentile, who ran a number of businesses, was as good as his name (pronounced *jen-TILL-ay*), and when he and Torry met for the first time, all it took was a hard, slow look between them and he gave her a signed blank check (literally) to take to the Lansing State Liquor Control Commission to complete the Del Rio business deal!

Also at that time Gentile handed an envelope to Torry, Ernie, and Rick, who counted $1,500 in cash, asked "What for?" in unison and when Phil explained that this was the monthly "kick-back" from the beer distributor, they looked at each other in quick inquiry and Torry handed back the envelope and said "No thank you," to Phil's consternation. The next week two very large, black-coated, steely-eyed "wrestlers" visited the Del Rio from Detroit and "explained" to Julie Detwiler why we "had to take the beer." Torry and Julie stared back and again said "No thank you," to the men's consternation, and offered them a parting drink!

The Harburgs and Burgess wanted a bar that would appeal to their friends—U-M grads, social activists, beatniks, artists. The bar they bought from Gentile had attracted a hard-drinking, blue-collar, almost solidly white male clientele. Part of the problem in appealing to a new group of customers was the old crowd and the old location. "The neighborhood was rough and tumble. I used to say I could read my book by the red light shining from the cop car," recalled Harburg.

In that first year the Del Rio neighborhood was a rough place to own a bar. There were occasional knifings. Independent hookers stayed at the Earle Hotel across the street from the Del Rio and came in and out on an old bus route between Paducah, Kentucky, and Ann Arbor. Its only stops were at the Willow Run Airport, east of Ypsilanti, and at the Earle Hotel across from the Del Rio. The hotel took in the transients and welfare people.

Cops were prevalent there in downtown Ann Arbor, which was suffering from urban decay. It was a time when most cities dealt with the problem by tearing down the old buildings. But the stately structures in the Del Rio block hid beautiful brickwork under their cracking paint. With new thinking, rebirth was possible.

The first changes had come to skid row in 1969 when Ned Duke and Buddy Jack opened a neighborhood bar called Mr. Flood's Party. It was a wild musical museum full of students, hippies, and a boogie beat. Duke was a collector of wonderful stuff and he used the bar to house his collection. Thirty Tiffany lamps shone from the ceiling, a statue of a monk stood on the end of one long table, an antique barber chair stood inside the ornate wooden doorway, and a moosehead kept glass eyes on drunken revelers. Local bands played on a high stage by the front door. The music ranged from blues to bluegrass to country swing.

Mr. Flood's was always full and when the Del Rio opened, some of the crowd trickled down the block to check out this new bar. The Del Rio had no cover charge because the music was on tape, but what music it was! Charlie Parker, Jimi Hendrix, John McLaughlin, Bach, Zappa, Miles and Vivaldi—stuff you wouldn't hear at any other place in town at the time.

Rick owned an incredible collection of LP's and had transferred much of it to tape. Thousands of hours of 8-tracks covered part of the wall behind the bar. Six foot tall Klipschorn speakers and a sophisticated amplifier meant clarity and sometimes heart-thumping volume.

The dramatic renovations to the interior of the building, done at the "barnraising" gave notice that something new was coming. The new owners soon ripped out the jukebox that had played hard rock and country tunes. Instead, on Sunday nights, Rick Burgess and other musicians performed *jazz at no charge.* And slowly but steadily, a different crowd was showing up—men with long hair, women in Indian woodblock skirts, and regular downtowners searching for a new place in the new times. *The Del Rio never advertised* but instead—successfully—relied only on word of mouth throughout its thirty-three-year life.

"A generation of counterculture folks started venturing out and liking it," said longtime customer Larry Hunter. Hunter's own visits to the Bar were signs of its transformation: an African-American, he had steered clear of the old Del, which clearly was unfriendly to both blacks and women. This old discrimination disappeared from the Del Rio Bar on day one. Harburg recalls sitting at a front table when an older black man entered with a very thin puzzled face. Ernie greeted him and invited him in. The man then admitted that the last time he had come here he was thrown out for being black. Ernie ordered him a beer and they had a good talk about the old days and the new bar. Rick's band, a tight group of blacks and whites, also brought in a diverse crowd.

The sixties in the nation and in Ann Arbor were marked by strikes and protests by activists against the established American culture of injustice and discrimination against blacks. Public dissent in Ann Arbor was shown with a picket/protest against the University of Michigan led by Charles Thomas, a black activist and dancer/actor, and later a Del Rio regular. Charles strode into the clerical halls of the university filled with all-white women with the police chasing him and he repeatedly projected his questions in a deep baritone, "Where are they? I don't see any! I don't see any! Where you hiding the black folk?" He and his mixed band of activists helped spread the protests to small businesses around Ann Arbor. Early in the sixties, a few town-and-gown dissenters also picketed for fair housing. The Black Action Movement strike of African-American students shut down the University of Michigan in 1970 to demand changes in racist policies at the university. By the mid-seventies a 100-year Jim Crow segregation in the city had been "opened up" to equality in public places and residential areas. The city "leaders" resisted but reluctantly yielded.

Within half a year of its opening, a new crowd had taken over the Bar. "And the fights between the old and the new crowds finally stopped, and we became a seventies place," recalled Harburg. "I can remember old-timers coming into the Bar, and they would hear music they hadn't heard and see people dressed as they hadn't seen," said Hunter.

Business was often so slow the first few months during the early seventies' recession that the owners developed a strategy: They would call up friends and beg them to come to the Bar. Once they arrived, "We told them they couldn't leave unless they got people to take their place," said Harburg. There finally came an evening when he was sitting at a table in the crowded, atmospherically dark room, with tapes of cool jazz playing, near a party of four young women. "They were talking about philosophy and their lives and their guys, with the candles going," he remembered. "And I said, 'Torry, I think we've made it.'" When the state lowered the drinking age to eighteen in 1971, there were lines at the Del Rio around the block. But Elvin, the great doortender, had to follow the new Del Rio Rule—made by the staff—*no one gets in without being able to sit at the bar or a table!*

The Del Rio Staff in the seventies. Torry and Ernie are second and third from left in the top row. Betty is second from right in the second row.

Elv is a big man with a big grin. His eyes twinkle beneath a high forehead and curly black hair. He looks like he could pick up a person with one hand, but he is a gentle giant. He drives a big custom Dodge van with a CB radio. His handle is Big Daddy and a sign on the back of the van says, "To know me is to love me."

Elvin keeps the Del Rio clean. His day starts at 8 a.m. when he enters the kitchen door, grinds beans for the day's first pot of coffee, and puts a tape in the sound system. The giant speakers come alive and the bar is filled with rhythm and blues while Elvin empties the trash and moves the chairs and tables aside to sweep and mop.

On Sunday afternoons Elvin is the doortender. It's his personal shift during the free jazz sessions. Elvin's big smile is the customer's first course in the Sunday Jazz Feast. Ev has a knack for making people feel welcome. The bar doesn't open until 5, but by 4:30 people are lining up outside the front door. Folks come from as far as Detroit for the experience.

The lights are lowered and the music begins. The crowd is musically transported to New York in the fifties, then maybe to a small Chicago club in the sixties. Sometimes an unscheduled musician will come in off the street and sit in with the band. Maybe a player will take a break to the kitchen for coffee while another takes off on an extended solo.

Elvin continues his greeting and seating, trying to get everyone in, stretching the limits of some tables, sometimes seating three different couples at one big table—turning strangers into friends. And still people wait outside for their turn. They hang there on the corner and watch the world pass by.

Elvin became a doortender because he was there to fill a need. When Sunday jazz first happened, it was the only time when more people wanted to be in the bar than the bar could accommodate. Someone had to be stationed at the door to slow the flow, and Ev was available that day. He enjoyed it and kept the shift. As other nights got busier, other people were needed to "work the door," and the job evolved.

The doortender is not a bouncer. The doortender is a facilitator of friendly flowings. The DT is the first person anyone entering the Del Rio sees, the one who helps set the mood of the place and the attitude of the customer.

A few years after the Del opened, the student newspaper, the *Michigan Daily,* approvingly described it as a place where "campus intelligentsia and pseudo intelligentsia hang out to discuss the heavy issues of the day." And "from its high tin ceiling to its shuttered windows to its live jazz on lazy Sunday afternoons," the review concluded, "the long narrow Del Rio is Ann Arbor's Greenwich Village saloon"—only without the then-overt sexism of the "saloons" in Manhattan, because this was Ann Arbor. The rule in the Del was strictly enforced: *No customer—male or female—could "hit on" another without permission of the "hitee"*! Once an irate lawyer called and threatened a law suit for having been refused service after his sexist behavior toward a waitperson; he backed off when Harburg suggested that the lawyer's wife, a former wait person in her career, probably would not support this law suit.

The Founders

Four unconventional people played crucial roles in shaping the Del Rio: Ernie Harburg, Torry Pedersen Harburg, Rick Burgess, and, starting the second year the Bar was open, bookkeeper and factotum Betty Vary. Very different personalities, they shared similar values and an unusual vision for the Bar.

Ernie Harburg is the son of renowned lyricist E.Y. "Yip" Harburg, who wrote the lyrics to, among others, all the songs in *The Wizard of Oz*, the Broadway musical *Finian's Rainbow,* and the classic Depression-era songs "Brother, Can You Spare a Dime?" and "It's Only a Paper Moon."[37] A lyricist of rare talent, who was posthumously acknowledged by the 2005 issuance of a Yip Harburg commemorative stamp, the senior Harburg was also a democratic socialist, a civil rights activist, and supporter of labor unions. He was blacklisted from films, TV, and radio in the fifties.[38] While Yip dodged the draft in 1917—as a socialist he was opposed to the war and went to Uruguay—Ernie served in the Army Air Force for two years (the good war) and shared his father's beliefs. While a graduate student at the University of Wisconsin, he had helped organize a union strike at the factory where he worked part-time. Harburg the son—tall, well spoken, and a raconteur with a decided New York style—is proud of being a nonconformist. He was pleased when his friend Jack Erfurt, a brilliant, red-bearded leading social activist in Ann Arbor (a dropout from the Law School), told a local newspaper, "Ernie was counterculture before the counterculture." This observation applied more to Jack, who was thrown out of the neuropsychiatric hospital (his way of avoiding the draft) for attempting to organize his fellow patients into a union! He then became Harburg's research associate on the Detroit project.

Former Bar employee (1989–1994), and now college instructor, Steve Auerbach described Harburg as "outgoing, real intelligent, with a great sense of humor. He loves to talk." Auerbach said that Harburg's welcoming speech, repeated to generations of new hires, captured the Del's spirit. With a look of delight on his face, Harburg informed them, "You are now a Delroid," and made it clear that the Bar owners would always ("for the rest of your life," he'd put it) be there for them. "If you need to, call collect. If you're in trouble, get on the red line, and we'll send the copter out to rescue you." The Del actually did rescue people from Taiwan, Windsor, and Mississippi by sending funds to beleaguered ex-staff!

Like Ernie, Torry Pedersen Harburg had an outgoing nature and a passion for righting societal wrongs. The two had met during World War II in the forties at progressive Antioch College in Ohio, and despite some differences in background (she was from Omaha, Nebraska, and he from Brooklyn, New York, and Brentwood, Los Angeles) found they were kindred spirits. This was a lucky thing, especially for Ernie, because at Antioch in 1944 there were only 25 males and 350 women! In fact, Torry had two roommates and all three made a personal list of men on campus—each stalked and married her number one choice! (Ernie and Torry stayed married for thirty-five years.) From her activist and socialist father and a mother who had gone to jail with Margaret Sanger in 1917 in New York City, Torry inherited a deep Midwestern integrity and a vision of an open, nonhierarchical workplace.

Like her parents, she was *incorruptible*. She became a reporter in Santa Monica (and Detroit) and an early sixties member of Ann Arbor Women for Peace, *which operated by consensus with no officers*. After the Del opened, when she had more time to spend in the Bar than Ernie, she often worked as a doorperson or even bartender, and her vivacity and bedrock honesty made her popular with the customers. "Torry was the life of the party," recalled Larry Hunter. "She was this willowy blonde with a great sense of humor." Torry Pedersen Harburg died in 1981 after 10 years with the Del Rio Bar, following a year-long struggle with cancer; she was mourned by many. On a corner of First and Liberty, in downtown Ann Arbor, a plaque adorns a tree dedicated in her honor to "an invincible spirit."

Rick Burgess is a man of few words, unlike the loquacious Harburgs, but he influenced the Bar in everything from its music to its appearance. "A holdover from the beatnik generation," Larry Hunter described Burgess. "He's always been the quintessential Mr. Cool," said Larry Behnke. "Rick speaks through his music." Eventually quitting his computer job, the short, bearded Burgess worked as a Del bartender in addition to playing jazz piano on Sundays. Rick liked dark places and the color black. This was why the lighting was toned way down, recalled Julie Detwiler. Because of Burgess, she remembered, the bar stools were re-covered in black and the Bar served coffee in black mugs, although "they were hard to find and expensive." Rick had a profound sense of atmosphere. He wanted the Bar to be dark. *"Nobody should see each other's face except in shadows and dreams"* and the tables should be narrow enough so that couples would sit only *"a kiss away from each other."*

Burgess made it clear early on, according to notes from old Del Rio meetings, that he wanted "musical control" of the Del. "You can't choose music by committee," he said later. Day to day, this meant that Burgess reigned over the more than 1,000 eclectic tapes (and later CDs)—from Chopin to Janis Joplin—that he organized and often played in the Bar. Tapes he hadn't selected were forbidden—an edict that the otherwise independent staff surprisingly accepted. They agreed to his musical choices because he was knowledgeable and was always open to suggestions for new music. One local paper in 1983 had this to say:

Jazz Tradition
by Jackie Young
Weekend, March 11, 1983

For at least a dozen years jazz lovers have been cramming the Del Rio Bar forming what jazz follower Ron Brooks calls "the Del Rio tradition."

Brooks, who is himself a talented jazz musician, has been in charge of rounding up jazz groups to play at the Del Rio for many years. Every Sunday evening a different jazz group is featured.

Finding different groups to play is not very difficult, according to Brooks. Musicians want to play the Del Rio because of its "enthusiastic jazz audiences which get both University and community support," he said. As a result, the Del Rio attracts a variety of musicians from across the state. "The intimacy of the setting is an important element to the musicians," he added.

And intimate the Del Rio certainly is! Usually the small bar floor is completely filled to capacity on Sunday evenings, with the wooden booths and tables packed in so tightly around the tiny 10-by-10 foot stage that it's sometimes hard to distinguish the audience from the musicians.

But the smallness of the room does not detract from the nightclubish atmosphere that pervades the bar. A conglomeration of wood shutters block out outside light and the room seems almost like a basement with the abstract paintings of jazz musicians adding a cultured touch to the red brick walls and old fashioned ceilings.

Brooks can recall jazz artists such as Stanley Cowel, Kenny Cox, Danny Spencer, and Larry Nozero playing at the Del Rio at some time. Some of Buddy Rich's band members have "sat in" on occasion, as have members of Duke Ellington's band, he said.

On one recent Sunday, local pianist Larry Manderville jammed with a group of musicians primarily from the Detroit area.

Manderville said he likes playing at the Del Rio "because everyone can hear what's happening." Manderville's group mellowed out the crowded bar room with a Miles Davis tune, "All Blues." A cold glass of California white wine or a pitcher of German beer could not have done the job better. Yet another piece—"Blues Bossa"—got the audience very much moving with its upbeat rhythm and powerful sax solos.

To Manderville, who plays with many different groups, the spontaneity of the jazz art form is a way of life. "Jazz is a lifestyle. You take one beat at a time and make the most out of it," he said. "It is good this way because you don't form an attitude on the song before you play it. You just play and you don't have time to form prejudices."

Whether you're a jazz expert or just an appreciator of musical creativity, the Del Rio has a lure for those who wish to be lulled by the swaying, foot tapping rhythm of good jazz music. But if you want to get a seat you better get there before 5pm Sunday. The small building is usually packed with patrons, some even lined up outside its doors on the corner of Washington and Ashley Streets, waiting to jam in the Del Rio tradition.

Burgess also had a philosophy: the music shouldn't drown out the customers' conversation, and it should fit the mood at that hour, which got louder toward midnight when the staff had its nightly toast of tequila!

Around midnight Mary brought in a special treat given to her by a friend: a bottle of Mezcal Con Gusano Monte Alban Regional de Oaxaca with Agave worm. Shots were poured, Ed was summoned from the kitchen, Elvin left the door station and with the rest of the crew, gathered around the wait station to toast, to Halloween, to craziness, to the joy of being able to run this wonderful institution in such a fashion. Down went the shots to various gags and groans. No one wanted the worm. To some it was supposedly an honor to get to eat the disgusting, pickled creature. To others the worm was there to soak up the toxins and impurities of the tequila. No one had to prove anything and no one ate the worm that night. It floated around the bottom of the bottle, alone and unwanted.

Near closing time it was nearly forgotten that it was Halloween. The occasional costumed customers had become commonplace and the River workers were tired and drugged, but happy. No traumas, no freak-outs, a good time was had by most. The night was a success.

Above all, Burgess established the free Sunday evening jazz sessions that characterized the Del for three decades. In the *Ann Arbor Observer*, critic Piotr Michalowski wrote, "The music changes from week to week, but everything else remains very much the same, including the listeners, many of whom have been coming [to the Del Rio] for years." Of one of them, he wrote, "Lou Crampton makes his way through the narrow room with the assistance of a walker, still enjoying the music in his eighth decade."

Ken Ishizu's involvement was short-lived—and nearly disastrous. As the Bar's manager, Ishizu was responsible for business details such as paying the taxes. One day about a year after the Bar opened, Harburg and Burgess arrived to find a notice on the door that the Bar had been closed by order of the IRS! "That was the first we knew about it," Harburg recalled. The partnership ended on the spot. So did the employment of Ishizu's waitress girlfriend, who did not take kindly to her termination. Like many Del Rio employees after, she was not shy about making her views known. Recalled Harburg: "She'd sit here at the end of the Bar cursing and swearing, because we gave her two weeks to get out." The taxes were then paid off daily by Rick who personally gave Mr. Chung of the Michigan IRS a piece of each night's income for several months. When the last of the taxes were paid off, Mr. Chung spoke and smiled for the very first time and gave the sage, "Confucian advice" to Rick, "Remember, remove the coins from the people." That night, the owners had a small celebration!

On the heels of Ishizu's departure, Betty Vary arrived. A friend of Torry Harburg, she came in as a bookkeeper. She had been the treasurer of the run for U.S. Representative Michael Stillwell, a short-lived Ann Arbor Peace candidate ("Stop the War!") and she came college-trained from a working-class family in Flint, Michigan. She was also a former grade school teacher, which Harburg claimed trained her for work at the bar. "It was supposed to be for six months," Vary recalled with amusement during the spring of 2002—thirty-two years later. In the early years Vary was not yet an owner, but she was a pivotal figure. Larry Behnke wrote, "The quiet Betty Vary exterior hid the financial dynamo that propelled the Del Rio enterprise through decades of ups and downs."

Besides keeping the books, Vary soon assumed a crucial behind-the-scenes role. *She coordinated communications between the Bar's owners and the employees*, troubleshooting and negotiating when necessary. Both sides trusted her completely. "Betty was always everyone's perfect mom, so kind and holding things together," said Tim Delaney, who worked at the Del for several years in the nineties. Betty was the "goodest den-mother."

"You won't find a sweeter person [than Betty]," said former bartender turned organic farmer/cook Danny Calderone. "We used to joke that Ricky bought the Bar to have a place to play his music, that Ernie bought it to have his own life-sized mouse maze—to see how people would react within the parameters of his eyes—and Torry was in it because she was a socialist and wanted to change the world. Betty just fit in because she loved being around people." But the owners and staff shared a common vision of the Bar's struggle for a democratic workplace.

"What an Exciting Time to Be in Ann Arbor"

Almost thirty years after she worked at the Del Rio in the early seventies, Julie Detwiler, fifty-nine, sat at a table in the former bar and shared her memories of an important time in her life. With her long, graying brown hair, her T-shirt featuring an abstract drawing, and dangling earrings in the shape of little Mexican sombreros, she looked like someone a longtime Ann Arborite would affectionately characterize as one of the city's many aging hippies.

Like many people who worked at the Del Rio in the early years, Detwiler came to Ann Arbor to attend U-M and dropped out, caught up in the chaotic days of the late sixties. And, like many of the employees during those years, she became estranged from her parents—whom she (accurately, according to other sources) described as "right wing and racist"— and found a replacement family among her fellow Delroids.

Detwiler, who has since worked on and off in restaurants over the years, recalls the excitement of the Bar's growing popularity. "At first it was just a big empty room," she said. Then, slowly but steadily, it seemed to transform. "It wasn't just old drunks that came in anymore, and it was a place to bring your kids. Everybody was welcome, no matter what color you were, what age you were. You could come in under age if you didn't order a drink. We observed the liquor control laws as if they were an act of nature." Most of the time.

The Evening of the Bust

It was Friday night, busy, crazy, usually the most hectic night at the Del Rio. The end of the work week brought out the people looking to unwind. Elvin was working the door, trying to control the flow, scurrying around trying to satisfy everyone's needs and moving just below the speed of sound.

The music thumped and whined a raucous urge to let go, pushing the partiers to higher levels of laughter and consumption. With pockets full of the week's pay check, they were apt to spend a bit more than any other night. Tommy and Tina kept the liquid flowing as fast as the waits and bar-sitters ordered it. Food flew from the kitchen as Ed and Char cranked their mighty cooking machine into high gear. The Del Rio was functioning at its peak.

Officers Burns and Steadly found a couple of seats at the bar in Tommy's section. They were wearing casual street clothes and they ordered beers. They didn't look at all like cops. Tommy served them with a smile, took their money, returned their change with a "Thanks," and rushed off to fill orders at the wait station.

At the front door Elvin was feeling the pressure. Too many wanted to get in with not enough places for them to sit. Next in line two young guys were ready for the table in Lenny's section that just cleared out. El was about to ask for their ID, but got called over to help Mary with a problem. They look old enough, he thought. He pointed them in the direction of the table and dealt with the group of three that had tried to rush in the door when his back was turned.

Lenny dropped off menus at the new table while on his way to the kitchen to pick up a big order for the round table of six. He served the food, then delivered the drinks he'd ordered to the booth of four, before returning to the two guys.

"Hi, what can I get for you tonight?" Lenny asked them. They didn't look him in the eye, but stared at their menus. Both ordered a draft beer.

For a split second Lenny thought he should check their ID, but damn! He was so busy and El probably checked them and "ding," that was his food pickup bell and well, these big guys with beard stubble certainly looked old enough for a couple of beers.

Lenny didn't see the two plainclothes police officers sitting at the bar not four feet away, eyeing his action at the table. On a slower night he might have picked up on their odd tension and furtive glances. Tonight he was lucky to remember to breathe. He brought the two beers to the table and went to the kitchen to put in an order for another table. When he returned to the floor, the two young men were gone, their beers were untouched, and standing next to the table were officers Burns and Steadly.

Burns blocked Lenny's path. "We're here to cite you for serving alcohol to minors," he said.

Lenny's heart sank. Oh, shit, he thought. Busted!

The rest of the encounter for Lenny was a blur, like a bad dream he tried to forget before it was over. The cops took down his name. Torry had been sitting at the front table, and came over to talk to the cops. Lenny cruised his section on automatic, trying to meet the needs of the many customers as though nothing had happened. But it had and Lenny felt that the entire bar was in trouble because of him.

Lenny continued his work and watched out of the corner of his eye as Torry did her official dance of duty with the cops. They handed her a piece of paper and left. That made him feel a little better. So did Mary when she came up and patted him on the back with assurances that it would work out OK. Tommy made a comment about "those assholes," and El came over to apologize for not checking the two guys' IDs at the door.

Talk that night at the Del Rio was about the bust. As the grapevine expanded, more information came to light. The Del Rio was not alone. *Twelve other bars and booze stores in Ann Arbor were also busted this same Friday night*. And it turned out that the young men who helped the police were Boy Scouts, from Explorer Post 155, which is sponsored by the city police!

The decoy booze busts were done, according to the Ann Arbor police chief, "in response to complaints from parents, citizens and state agencies." Employees serving booze to minors could be charged with a misdemeanor carrying a maximum penalty of 90 days in jail and a $100 fine. Repeat offenses meant closing down the bar.

Of the twelve Friday night busted businesses, some went to court to plead innocence. A jury listened to testimony by the Explorer Scouts. Defense arguments ranged from employees who felt they had made "adequate diligent visual inquiry" to "the drink served was not analyzed for chemical content, so there is no proof." In more than one case, a waitress said she was not told of the customer's age by the doorman.

The Del Rio bit the bullet and paid a fine. Lenny wasn't prosecuted this first time. A second offense would mean closing the bar for three days; further offenses would close the bar longer. The situation called for caution. A note went up on the Del Rio bulletin board the next day:

IMPORTANT

> I know you must be aware of being cited on Friday night. So we must be extremely careful. The doorperson must check all IDs. If we were to be closed down for 3 days, it would be a great financial loss. Thirty days would be a disaster. And we might not recover from being closed for 90 days.

There was much talk in the community about the decoy busts. The police maintained that they were only upholding the law. People in support of the police action commented in the *Ann Arbor News*, "It's about time the Boy Scouts are doing something besides walking old ladies across the street," and "I approve of any method to get rid of dishonest liquor salesmen."

On the other side, people wrote the *News*, "I thought Boy Scouts were supposed to be trustworthy," and "When police resort to hiring 'actors' in order to entrap people into committing a crime, I ask 'Who are the criminals and who are the real offenders?'"

The Del Rio staff remained vigilant. They may have been living a lifestyle of snubbing authority, but when a certain authority can take away your playground *and* your source of income, it's time to pay serious attention and play by the rules.

Creative Detburgers and Marital Stuff

Julie Detwiler smiled when she described the creation of the Del Rio's popular "Detburger," which the *Washington Post* once rated as one of the twenty best hamburgers in the country. Her former husband, Bob "Det" Detwiler, now deceased, was a bartender and a purist jazz pianist; one night, four regular customers begged him to "cook us something different." Det—somewhat under the influence—went back into the kitchen and experimented—and it was made this way:

> *Patty on grill, bun under cover of grill, flip patty, cover with mushrooms, green peppers, and black olives, splash beer on top, throw on a slice of cheese, cover to steam, put onions on bottom bun, put top bun on burger, cover briefly to soften, set on bottom, and serve with pickle spear and chips.*

Detwiler also spoke of personal turmoil. She and her husband broke up during the years she worked at the Del, and she recalled serving customers with tears streaming down her face. "Customers would ask, 'Are you okay?' and I'd say, 'No, I'm not okay, but I can still serve you.'" She remembered standing in the kitchen, weeping, her concerned co-workers hugging her and saying, "Julie, we all want to help you." The Del was to become the scene of several staff "divorce parties" after Julie's. But there were also marital sendoffs. Our scribe notes:

> *Monday morning the bar was buzzing with the news: Mary and Roger were getting married. They'd been a happy item for some months and felt like it was time to make a more traditional commitment. For many at the Del Rio, this was a sacrilege. You don't need that piece of paper, some said; just live together. Cohabitation was the accepted method of "marriage" for the young and hip. Now why would Mary and Roger want to get married and destroy a beautiful friendship?*
>
> *Perhaps our young lovers had a sentimental relapse or a nostalgic bout with something they felt more lasting. Whatever the case, they were serious.*

They were getting married and would very much like to have the ceremony at the Del Rio on a Sunday (before the place was open, of course). They requested the date at a monthly meeting and it was approved by all. No one could turn down a chance to party.

A week before the event, a list went up on the bulletin board. The wedding would be potluck. "Who could bring a dish to share? Please write it down below. Thanks." Over the next couple of days a list materialized:

Rick would provide a roast turkey. A Finnish salad extraordinaire would be made by Tina. Joy would bake a batch of cookies. Charlotte signed to bring fruit salad. Ed would bake whole wheat rolls. Barb, curried rice with chicken. Lenny, Waldorf salad. Julie, Spanish rice casserole. Tommy, potato salad. Elvin, a variety of bags of chips. Pete, a veggie casserole. And Ernie assured everyone there would be plenty of champagne for the celebration.

Last year, in an attempt at becoming draft exempt, Tommy had sent for clergy membership in the Church of Universal Life. Although he never planned on performing clerical duties, he was now a legally ordained minister and sure, he'd be happy to officiate at the wedding.

The day dawned fresh and sunny. It was a perfect Sunday, made for love and lovers. The Del Rio family arrived in the mood to celebrate. The strangeness of one of them getting married was replaced by the optimism and joy of the gathering.

Bob Marley was on the tape machine, needlessly urging, "you got to lively up yourself." Smiles and laughter filled the bar. Lively colors merged with long hair as folks dressed up in their finest party clothes. Whether it was a newly tie-dyed T-shirt or a long, flower-print granny dress, an India print shirt or skirt, or bell bottoms with bright new patches and beads and dangly earrings, the gang looked good.

Friends and relatives of the bar workers, especially Mary and Roger's family, met and mingled with the others. People couldn't stop smiling. When it looked like everyone had arrived, Tommy cleared his throat.

"Could I have your attention, please," he yelled above the din. "We're happy to have you all here today in celebration of Mary and Roger's wedding." Hoots and whistles and clapping eventually died down and the ceremony began.

Mary and Roger stood across from Tommy at the front of the bar where sunlight streamed in the window and formed halos around the three of them. Both Mary and Roger held flowers and each other's hands. They listened to Tommy's short reading with peaceful looks on their faces, then exchanged simple homemade vows. It was nothing like the traditional "love, honor and obey," but more like "love, listen to, and respect." Most of the words were lost on the crowd, but the attitude came through.

The ceremony ended quickly, the couple kissed, hugged and turned to the audience who rushed them with hugs and well-wishes. With the formal business out of the way, the crowd could get down to some serious partying.

Champagne corks popped and flew across the room. The Doors sang the musical question, "Do you love her madly?" Roger answered with the first champagne toast to his new bride, "I do!"

The food dishes on the large table were uncovered and the feasting began. The front doors opened and some people spilled out onto the street corner. Joints were lit and passed, but drinks were left inside the bar (no alcohol was allowed outside the bar and no pot was allowed inside the bar; they knew their proper places).

A passing cop car slowed down to have a better look at this wild gathering. Two policemen got out and walked up to the front door. Ernie rushed to meet them. "May I help you officers?" They wanted to see the Del Rio liquor license and make sure that the bar was not open for business. That would have been illegal. Ernie assured them that this was a closed wedding party and the bar would not open until its regular Sunday time of 5:00. They appeared satisfied and soon left. The hastily stubbed-out joints were re-lit and the partying continued. Chuckles and jokes about the cops saving us from ourselves passed among the revelers.

Since Rick's band had planned on playing that evening for Sunday Jazz, they had set up early and commenced playing. Some tables were pushed back and a dance floor emerged to claim boogie buddies bumping to the beat. Mary and Roger danced slow and close until others cut in and took a spin with the newlyweds.

Tinker, dressed in his finest rainbow crocheted suit, took a turn dancing with Mary. He joked that since she and Roger had met at the Del Rio and were married at the Del Rio, perhaps they should also have their honeymoon here and (in the privacy of the basement, of course) conceive their first child at the Del Rio. Mary gave Tinker a playful bonk on the head and went back to dancing with her new husband.

Mary and Roger did eventually leave on their honeymoon, but it was not at the Del Rio. They spent a few days at a cottage at an unspecified lake a couple of hours north of Ann Arbor.

After they'd left, everyone pitched in to clean up all evidence of the grand celebration that had taken place on that happy warm Sunday.

The next day, people who came into the bar saw this note on the bulletin board:

Del Rio Family . . .

Thanks are not enough to say how happy and grateful we are to you all for the beautiful "start" you've given us, so . . . we'll see you soon.

Love, Mary and Roger

In 1982 Ernie and his new wife Deena were married in the Bar, with a twenty-champagne-bottle salute! At that time Ernie put up a sign for the ceremony, which lasted to the Bar's demise, paraphrased from e e cummings: "Beside the ever-lasting 'why' and 'maybe,' there is the Absolute YES!" Harburg felt it applied to all honest commitments.

Ernie and Deena—Del Rio wedding day

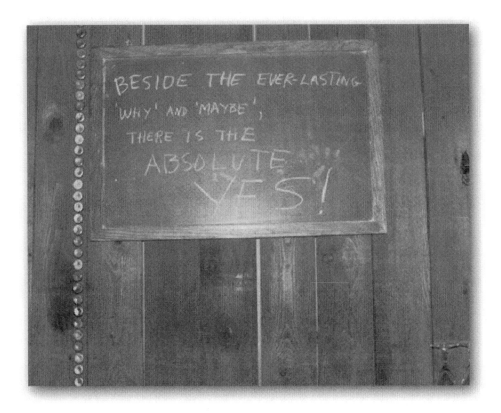

A Magical Time

Detwiler and the others were living out their personal dramas during an extraordinary period in American history—and in a city that, more than most, reflected the changing times. At some point, it became impossible to separate the Bar from the city of Ann Arbor, which had become one of the national hotbeds of anti-Vietnam war activity[39]—the "teach-in" was started at the University of Michigan—and a thriving counterculture scene. Antiwar protests in Ann Arbor occasionally resulted in clashes between police and students. In the streets, strangers flashed the peace sign at each other, and there was a lot of excited, if vague, talk about "revolution." "Underground papers" flourished: the *Ann Arbor Argus* (White Panthers) morphed into the *Ann Arbor Sun* (Rainbow People's Party—all colors), plus there was a women's paper and others. A Free People's (medical) Clinic opened its doors, and the first citywide "Hash Bash"—which would become a tradition—promoted legalization of marijuana. In 1974, the city's voters, no longer predominantly Republican, approved a $5 fine for possession of marijuana, to replace the stricter state penalties.

"What an exciting time to be in Ann Arbor," recalled Larry Behnke. "So much was going on—not only protests and demonstrations, but art and film. It was incredible." A few of the Del Rio staff had helped start and were part of a film group whose showing of *Flaming Creatures* on the campus was raided by Ann Arbor police for containing scenes of "frontal nudity." Once, Alice, a regular customer and self-proclaimed lesbian alcoholic, seriously offered to immolate herself as the Buddhist monks were doing in Viet Nam to protest the war—but she wanted to accomplish this in front of the Del Rio Bar! It took several days for Torry and Ernie to persuade Alice to drop this peace action from her agenda. (Alice later became a sober Ph.D. professor of language at a large university.) But her commitment to oppose a wrong war echoed through Ann Arbor and the nation, and the poet said:

> We learn this after every war
> That life is not worth dying for.[40]

The Del Rio became a gathering place for groups such as the Students for a Democratic Society and Ann Arbor Women for Peace. The Del was also popular with counterculture "pub singer" Patti Smith, whose occasional visits with her husband Fred, of MC5 fame, gave Delroids a thrill. "We had what we called 'the intellectual, funky place,'" said Harburg.

Graffiti and Talk Truth to Power

The graffiti was also more than just the normal raunchy sex invitations. For example:

Machismo is a social disease.

Easter has been called off, they found the body.

Cleanliness is next to Nothing.

Certainty is a hallucination.

Chanticleer is certain that every morning his crowing makes the sun come up.

The other part of the Del Life was more personal:

In the women's toilet was scrawled: "I look in the night mirror, drunk, having fought through the billowing clouds of disorder and discover . . . the gleaming and peaceful half moon of myself."

On the men's room wall: "The mystery of life is not a problem to be solved, but a reality to be experienced."—Alan Watts

Larry reports:

Sitting on the toilet she nearly forgot what she'd come in for. The dark pink wall in front of her totally grabbed her attention. It was covered with writings and drawings. Near the toilet paper dispenser a marking pen sat on a cradle of two nails. Above it was written, "Please feel free to make your mark on this wall!" Quite a few already had—not just sayings, but poems and drawings, quotes from popular songs, jokes and cartoons. Here in the toilet's locked solitude people had laid bare their feelings and given vent to creative urges. It was all too wonderful for Barb. She stared for quite a while before picking up the marker and writing, up above a peace sign with feet, an old Zappa lyric aimed at parents: "All your children are poor unfortunate victims of systems beyond their control, a plague upon your ignorance and the gray despair of your ugly life." No, Barb wasn't getting along well with her parents. She felt good leaving the quote on the wall and decided to read some of the other scribblings.

"I came in here to wash the puke off my face. Just thot I'd say Hi."

34

"I am a Black woman who is struggling thru a society, carrying a double load. I am using the method of love, understanding, and the knowledge of peace to get thru life, but if that doesn't work, I'm going to start kicking some ass!"

"The art of giving is the key to living."

"I'm so High I'm profound!"

"Let me live with laughing girls with shining eyes, high on life and living."

"What can you say when you're all blown out? Do you scream and dance, jump and shout? Waiting for your mind . . . "

"Marriage is one of the prime causes of divorce."

"We are the people our parents warned us about."

"Today I talked to an old friend and found out about you . . . and when winter reaches to put out the last fire, I will remember the spring that was Brenda."

"Our cause is righteous; our people are real; our goal is obtainable—Peace."

"There has to be a revelation before there can be a revolution."

Barb tried several times to leave the bathroom, but there was always one more entry that caught her eye, that kept her reading. Finally there was a knock on the door and she was transported back to pre-wall reality. "OK, I'm finished." She opened the door.

Joy was waiting outside and smiled at Barb. "I was worried; I thought you'd fallen in."

"Ha, ha. Just watch out for the wall," Barb warned. "It can be addicting." When Barb rejoined the group around the fire, the energy level had risen. So had the euphoric cloud, the group high that comes from sharing pot and sucking down draft beer.

The nearby Yippie bar, Mr. Flood's Party, which opened shortly before the Del, was considered edgier, less intellectual, but more popular media-stereotype counterculture, and more into heavy-duty drinking and light drug use. Another downtown bar, the Blind Pig—to which the Del loaned start-up funds —catered to heavier stuff and more "in-your-face" politics.

The Del was so inclusive that a couple of months after it opened, several gay men who hung out at the nearby unique Flame Bar came over and, Harburg recalled, "offered us their whole clientele," if they could be allowed to redecorate. (The men had issues with the Flame's owners.) The Del owners turned them down, emphasizing that the Del catered to an "open society," which included both gays and straights. Later in the mid-seventies, when a lesbian group made the same offer, it received the same response in a private meeting with Torry. They all agreed that the Del *welcomed and respected all people—provided they behaved courteously to all others.*

Recently three young men had come in wearing military dress whites. When Lenny walked over to take their order, one young guy looked up, wide-eyed and said, "Did you know that bar across the street is for queers?!"

They'd gone into the Flame Bar, an Ann Arbor institution, a place gays felt comfortable. The closer it got to closing time, the more gays would visit the Flame. The young soldiers, symbols of virile American manhood, had inadvertently met their antithesis and they were shaken. At the Del Rio they relaxed and as the darkness soothed and swallowed them, they laughed and told "queer" jokes. Not too far away from them, but out of their sight, two women sat together and kissed passionately.

Some other customers were just a little far out:

Clyde walked in and sat at the bar. His hair was disheveled and hung in his eyes. He was wearing a blue mechanic's uniform left over from his time as a fine fixer of cars. He was still a good mechanic, but no longer held a job. He lived with his parents and received disability payments. Someone said he'd been a brilliant mathematician, but took too much LSD and has never been the same. He did act peculiar, but often made sense, too.

Tina came over to take his order and he said, "'By George!' said Paul, as he sat on the John. 'Where did my Ringo?'"

"That's cute, Clyde," said Tina. "What can I get you?"

"Have no fear, I think it's clear, a beer would be dear." His face got all grinny and his eyes closed.

When Clyde spotted Ed, he leaned toward him and got serious. "Extract the negative," he said. "Don't seek the positive—it will come of its own accord when the negative is extracted."

Ed smiled at him. Some people thought Clyde was crazy, but harmless. Del Rio staff who'd gotten to know him treated him as any regular. They were polite as long as Clyde was cool, and the only problem they ever had with him was when he was too drunk. Even then he was happy and it was easy to walk him to the front door and tell him it was time to go home. Clyde would smile and raise his finger and say something like, "There *is* no wrong. When someone's negative, form a positive buffer. All right, the sight, I light, goodnight!" And off he'd walk down the street, heading for home.

The Del staff shared a general mistrust of the neocon U.S. government, and a number of the majority women employees identified with the fledgling women's and gay liberation movements. And like children of America's middle class everywhere, Del Rio employees were experimenting with drugs and with sexual freedom in ways that shocked their parents. The media fanned talk about the "generation gap." Recalled Larry Behnke, "A lot of us were rejecting our regular families. I loved my mother, but she didn't like my long hair and she didn't like it that I smoked pot." He found a substitute family, he said, among his fellow Delroids—and a brief time of his life to "drop out" and "satisfy his soul," as Walt Whitman put it. Harburg observed that the "straight-laced" media and parental wannabees would still call them "slackers" because one "must" go in linear, nonstop from school to a corporate career to be perceived as "normal."

Sex and the Del Rio Bar

"It was a magical time," Behnke continued, "between the invention of the birth control pill and the advent of AIDS." Sex within the Del Rio tribe was common—and Behnke said that it didn't lead to particularly strained relationships between co-workers. "It was hard to feel possessive about your sex partners, because there were so many of them." The bathrooms sold condoms of all shapes and colors. But naturally there were faux romantic ties wherein our poet's wisdom was ignored:

> Oh, innocent victims of Cupid,
> Remember this terse little verse:
> To let a fool kiss you is stupid,
> To let a kiss fool you is worse.[41]

One day a large sheet of paper was tacked up on the bulletin board. Over the next few days it was filled up and expanded. It said:

THE GREAT DEL RIO SEX SURVEY—
Where Did You First "Do It?"

(for real, now . . . names aren't necessary)
In a gay friend's executive apartment with works—bar, dinner, etc.
My girlfriend's bedroom in Jackson
On an old couch in my mother's basement (she was upstairs, too)
In a motel on Woodward Avenue
In a cabin up north—it was cold!
An apartment on Glen and Catherine Streets, on the bottom bunk
In a bush—Ouch!
In a drive-in movie; I got caught!
In a Rambler on its fold-down seat
Do what?

Oh, um . . . I can't remember. Do you mean willingly?
My friend's mother's bedroom
In San Francisco
In the Goodyear blimp
In an El Camino
Who's "It?"
In the back seat of a 1944 Ford
In a boring bedroom, and the woman was having her period
In an apartment in Montreal with a New Zealander (I did not remove a single article of clothing, including my underwear)
It was with two women . . . and a lava lamp, in a front parlor, and one's parents came home early . . . sad, but true
On her living room couch while her dad slept in the next room!
On a kneading table in a bakery
I'll tell you when it happens!
In my '62 Pontiac with the power steering and adjustable seats, power of course, along Huron River Drive
While piloting an airplane above a pinkish-orange cloud deck as the sun set in the west and full moon rose in the east

OK, then,
Where was the STRANGEST Place you ever "Did it?"

In a funeral home with a night watchman
On top of my van
On top of a clothes washer on the spin cycle
On the floor of a scorpion-infested jungle
On the roof of my sister-in-law's house
At a free concert
Driving down a highway in Canada with the woman waving at passing truckers
In the driver's seat of a VW bug, just to see if we could (in front of a cemetery)
On a secluded Lake Michigan dune that a cop later told us was not as secluded as we had thought
On the toilet in my mother's house, while my mother was in the living room
In the women's bathroom in the Del Rio

That's all well and good,
but Where Would You Like to "Do it?"
Fantasy time . . .

In the glass elevator of Detroit's Renaissance Center
In a very high tree house overlooking a lake
On a Ferris wheel
In a bed!
In a hot-air balloon over the ocean
In a cottage by the sea with a blanket on a breezy, moonlit night
In a vat of chocolate
On a large pizza with triple mushrooms

The Del Rio staff in Fall 1978

From the vantage point of middle age, Betty Vary tried to urge some caution among the Del staff. Once she and Torry posted a notice that read, "It has come to our attention that lately there have been a few 'accidents' involving Del Rio employees. This has made Torry and me feel remiss in our duties as the Del Rio mothers . . . therefore, a discussion will be held entitled 'How to Avoid the Making of a Baby.'"

Despite the warnings, some Del Rio single women did become pregnant. Before abortion became legal in Michigan with the 1973 Supreme Court *Roe v.Wade* ruling, *the Bar paid* for women to take the "Detroit cure" or even to fly to New York to terminate their pregnancies. (The abortions cost $800, travel included.) Those women who did give birth shunned hospitals and had their babies delivered at home. Several Del Rio women used the same midwife. The single mothers continued working at the Bar; often the kids attended monthly meetings. *Hours worked were scheduled by each work group and allowed full flexibility*—even to ex-Del people passing through town. In fact, the Del Rio had four categories for workers: "regulars," who had to have at least two shifts; "back-ups," who were on special case; "irregulars" and "drifters." For years, unlike all other bar-restaurants, there were practically no failures to show up for work, as the rule was *you either had to get a replacement or get your butt in*! This really worked when "enforced" by fellow workers.

Employee drug use fit the permissive tone of the time. People smoked pot in the downstairs basement and in the kitchen, where the pizza oven had a very effective ventilation system. "I'm going to the pizza oven" was code for "I'm going to smoke a joint." Former waitress and later teacher Diane Black (1972–80 and 1984–90) recalled more than one occasion when she had to prepare someone's order herself because the cook was outside on a pot-smoking break. "The popularity of pot made for a very mellow Bar, not only at times with the occasional stoned customers but occasionally with those staff members who smoked during their shift," wrote Larry Behnke, who went on to make a living as a writer and photographer in Florida on a weekly newspaper that he and his wife started up. Although staff was repeatedly reminded at meetings that drug use on the premises could close the place down, the warning had little effect.

Authority figures in general were not cool with the Delroids. On one early-seventies occasion when the Bar was closed, someone knocked, and a waitress opened the door to see a couple of men wearing suits and ties. She shouted "We don't serve capitalist pigs!" and slammed the door. Ernie Harburg laughed at this memory but called it an aberration. The Bar's tolerance, he said, enveloped everyone who came to the door. Still, though not common, the door slamming expressed a general mistrust of authority—and "authority" could sometimes include "suit and tie" and "skirt" customers. Former customer Pat Behnke (then-wife of Larry Behnke) recalls that in the mid-seventies, the Del staff's attitude sometimes amounted to arrogance. "They let you know if you were leaving a lousy tip," she recalled. Actually, the occasional in-your-face-stance was part of the Del's charm, she said. The regulars tipped generously.

Many on the Del Rio staff were strong individualists to start with—often college grads who shunned traditional careers. Larry Behnke, for example, graduated from U-M, took a conventional job for a year, and then turned his back on the traditional workforce to immerse himself in the Del Rio. Trained in art, he lived in a converted bread van painted in bright, psychedelic colors; he parked (rent free) around the Del and produced beautifully decorated menus and posters. In the charged, defiant atmosphere of Ann Arbor in the early seventies, it was easy for Behnke and others to decide they didn't want a manager. Said Behnke, "Our slogan was 'Power to the People'—we felt it and lived it." He himself was a true "flower power" peacenik and always a gentle man.

How to Run a Bar Without a Manager, As Reported by Larry Behnke

It was at one of the meetings at Julie's house that it was decided by most of the workers that Julie would no longer be the manager. Torry and Betty, who kept the books, were there, but they were careful not to push opinions; rather, they guided the discussion over rough spots. Mary worked many days with Julie and felt she could manage as well as Julie. Lenny made managing decisions without offending anyone and got away with it. Tommy didn't like anyone else telling him how to work. Charlotte didn't mind the way things were, but was adaptable. Tina was getting high on the controversy. Julie, like most of her co-workers, wasn't really sure what direction they were going in. It wasn't very comfortable for her, but it was certainly interesting.

"I'm not sure we need a manager any more," said Mary. "We do all the work."

"But, you don't always do what needs doing," said Julie. "And I have to do it."

"Well, who appointed you?" asked Tommy. He already knew no one had.

"Julie seems to be doing a good job," said Charlotte.

"We all do," said Mary. "Why do we have to have a MANAGER?!"

"Maybe we could try it without a manager for a while," said Torry.

"But we need a manager!" (That's the way it's always been done.)

"Well then, who will be the manager?" (Surely someone has to be in charge.)

"Well, we don't need a manager!" (Down with that parental authority crap!)

"We'll ALL be managers!" (Peace and Love Forever!)

At first, manager Julie Detwiler was replaced by consensus by two "coordinators." But according to meeting notes, even the position of coordinator had disappeared by the fall of 1974. Essentially, the Del Rio collective had divided itself into five groups: the waiters, or "waits"; the bartenders or "barts"; the door tenders or "dorts" (who checked IDs and helped seat people); the cooks; and the owners, nicknamed the "I/O," or "inside-outside group" because they were called upon to deal with outside issues of, say, taxes or the Michigan Department of Public Health—and keep the "books." Only Betty was trusted—and rightly so. Audits by IRS and the Liquor Control Commission had each found her records spotless! This was a minor miracle in a small bar, cash-only business!

Whatever the job description, all the employees *gathered regularly on the second Sunday of each month (for years to come)* to discuss the intricacies of running a Bar outside the traditional management structure. The meetings themselves were at first raucous affairs. Ernie Harburg recalls, "We'd have wine and cheese and we used to yell at each other until finally we learned how to modulate our voices and be courteous." Even how to conduct the meetings was debated. Eventually, it was decided to have one person "facilitate" the meeting and another take notes. An *open agenda* for the meeting was hung on the kitchen wall for everyone to add to. Every person at Sunday meetings was encouraged to—and did—speak up, and *only one person was allowed to speak at a time*. It was agreed that anyone who wanted to talk made a hand gesture to the facilitator who then called on them to speak in the order made by whomever gestured; but *no one was allowed to interrupt the person speaking—or else everyone objected to the "interrupter."* Everyone listened—really listened—to the person speaking. Newcomers served as "facilitator" or "notetaker" for a month, trained by Torry.

During the first year of Sunday meetings, the notes kept were more formal because it was all so new. Notes were like laws that were referred back to for guidance. As time passed the meeting notes grew less formal.

Charlotte offered to keep notes for this month's meeting. Her notes were snippets of conversation applied to paper:

Now, should Tina get sick pay? No, she quit, then came back. Listen, what we need here is a group of people who know what they're doing and this woman does; she put in two years and I think she deserves it. But we have a rule. Rules can be bent. Well, does anyone really object? OK, Tina gets sick pay.

Loans. Three people want one. How much do we have? There's $350 in the kitty. Mary wants $150 to go to Greece. Pete wants some for Arizona and Joy needs some for expenses. Well, Mary might not need that much. Good, 'cause we need to keep some for advances. So let's split it four ways, OK? Agreed.

Now Barb wants sick pay. Anyone object? She's not even here today. All right, we'll defer the item 'til she shows up.

The phone bill. We made an agreement to not use the business phone for personal long distance calls. So, pay your bills! And don't let customers use it. They can use the pay phone in back. We ought to be bold enough to tell people to hang up when they're tying up the phone. Put a sign on the phone. OK.

Checking IDs. Ohhh! Well, the scenario's gonna be that the cops won't do anything for a while, then they'll pick a victim and say they're just doing their job. Do we want the Del Rio to be the victim? No. Check IDs at the door! What about younger kids who don't drink? We'll stamp their foreheads with iridescent paint if they're not old enough. Hah! We can let them in, but we can't serve them. Some bars don't even let them in. People will pour shots of booze in their younger friends' Cokes. We need a sign at the door just to inform them not to be nasty or assume they'll rip us off. That would encourage it happening and they'll be drinking here in a couple of years anyway. So we should check IDs and be firm, but nice about it. OK.

What about that guy Lionel and his girlfriend; should they be barred? Arrgh! That jerk! He's out the door! Really! Yeah! OK, he's barred for sure.

Imported bottled beer. Should we investigate it more? We don't need it. Keep the money here. They don't recycle those bottles anyway. But, it's better. Someone who wants it check on it. OK.

Bad checks. Arrgh! It's mostly Fred Walker. He owes us $190. We couldn't get that much for advances! I talked with him, said *we were appalled and asked if he could pay us back a little each week. Hey, we're not even supposed to take checks! If you take a check, sign it and pay out of your pocket if it comes back bad. Right, we don't take checks here.*

Hey, it's time to get our group picture taken. OK, taller people in the back. This is Jesse, our photographer. Hi! Everybody say "Marijuana!"

Back to Barb's sick pay. She's here now. What's our policy? We get three quarters of regular pay. She's asking for 26 hours worth. Anyone object? OK, she's got it. Thanks; I'd like to thank everyone for your love and help. Yeah!

Pouring shots. Some bartenders are pouring doubles. Tommy's a little heavy on them. Tina does well. Guys, watch your shots, OK?

Bar lights. Sometimes it's too light in here at night. Yeah, I can still see my hand. Really, keep them low. Good.

Wages. Yeah, they're too low. We're working on it. Oh, I'm disgusted; it takes so long. Good things take time. The River Del is deep and wide. Well, come to the finance meeting and talk about wages. They don't change by themselves. It's up to us. Ain't nobody here but us chickens.

Can we go now? Anything else? No. Yippee! Go play, kids. End of meeting. Notes by Charlotte.

"All helped the newcomers to learn the Del culture," said Harburg. It took several meetings for these new people to believe their opinions helped run the Bar even if they had worked before for other "cooperatives." *The Del was a collectively run consensual affair.*

Out of necessity, the staff made some compromises with the Liquor Control edicts. For example, it was decided that in a stressful situation, the front bartender could claim to be manager. In an especially serious matter—for example, if the police were summoned—one of the owners would be called in. Never happened!

Del Rio Staff, late seventies

It took longer to make decisions about hiring and firing. Eventually, flexible guidelines, not hard-line policy, mandated that *new employees would be hired in open meetings of their employee group* (waits, barts, etc.) and given a three-month probation period. If the group decided their work was unsatisfactory, it could decide against hiring them. If the particular employee group was satisfied, then all the Del employees at the monthly meeting decided whether or not to hire them. When the cooks really did hire a blind man [true!] or the Ethiopian who refused to cook meat, the Bar was able to fire them after only a few days! It was also agreed that it was necessary to have a "head cook" to coordinate the kitchen work who would be paid more for this role. Margaret Parker, who first took on this challenging role, is now an Ann Arbor artist and art organizer. Behnke wrote:

Char discovered that there was no manager to hire new workers, rather a hiring meeting where any workers could attend to help jointly select their new co-worker. It was to be held next Tuesday afternoon when the lunch rush was over. When that day came Char was feeling really nervous. She even considered not going and facing all those people. It was almost too intimidating, but the idea of working at the Del Rio part time was what carried her through. She knew she could do the job as well as anyone.

Three other potential cooks came to sit at the table, as did maybe half the Del Rio workers who straggled in and filled up the remaining seats, then pulled nearby chairs closer. Char and the others wrote their names and phone numbers and a brief personal sketch on pieces of paper. Torry spoke a little about how the Del Rio manager-less system worked and what was expected of the workers.

"You may think it's cool not to have a manager," Torry said, "but it means you have more responsibilities because it's like we're all managers here. It's really a different gig. I know it's confusing and it may take six months before you can absorb most of the stuff already in the nervous systems of the other workers."

It didn't take long to interview the potential cooks. Each one told why they wanted to work at the Del Rio and what experience they had that qualified them. After each had a chance to talk they were told they could leave and would be called that day with the news, good or bad.

The next part of the hiring process sometimes took less time than the interviews. Because consensus was the method, if anyone strenuously objected to any of the applicants, that person would be ruled out. But it would have to be a good reason, not "I don't like her clothes," or "He was short with me once when I waited on him."

Charlotte was one of the two remaining cook applicants left after the first round of talks. It was agreed that they both had good qualifications. Now it was a matter of personal preferences. Arguments were made, opinions got hardened and softened as the big ripples smoothed to a more serene stream of collective agreement.

The remaining contenders were discussed for as long as it took for everyone to agree. The aggressive workers sometimes pushed their opinions at the beginning, but the shyer ones always had a chance for input, too. This was a serious matter. Hiring someone new was like choosing a member of the family. This person had to fit in with the style of the bar and be dependable. During the busiest times the Del Rio team of the moment functioned as a well-oiled machine, so it was important to choose someone who would aid that process, not slow it down. Intuitions played as large a part in hiring as did rational considerations. It also helped if someone already knew an applicant.

People at the Del Rio had gotten to know Charlotte and they liked her. It was finally agreed that she would best fill the job. The workers at the round table were relieved that once again consensus had worked, despite varying degrees of approval for the choice.

On the day of the lunch Char came to the Del Rio to meet with Ernie, Torry, and Betty. It was tradition to meet on neutral ground and today they would eat at the Cracked Crab restaurant only a half block away.

When they were seated and had ordered, Torry began the crash course. "Well, once a month we have a meeting like that," said Torry, "and we hope everyone shows up. It's where we decide how we run the bar. Sometimes we meet more often if something special needs deciding, but that monthly Sunday meeting is big stuff. We all decide on policies and then try our darndest to follow through with our decisions."

"It has its flaws and we're still learning," said Ernie, "but it's amazing how well it can work."

"We try to be positive about it," said Betty. She thought about some of the problems with the process. Power trips by some, others eating or drinking too much free stuff, some not using common sense—these incidents were in the minority, though. She had to admit that more often than not it was a wonder that all these different people together could be responsible enough to make it work.

"Sometimes it's a real challenge," said Torry, "but it's really satisfying, too."

Drawing by Larry Behnke

Once hired, *the employee could be fired only by a consensus of the Del Rio collective.* But firings turned out to be much more problematic than hirings. Throughout the Del Rio's unconventional history, firing was probably the action that employees shirked the most—even if someone was slacking off or getting drunk on the job. Once, recalls Betty Vary, it took three long, emotional meetings to fire an alcoholic employee whose work habits were giving his fellow workers grief. "It was like firing your brother or sister!" It took many months to fire one bartender who had mesmerized his fellow workers while secretly pushing drugs using Bar money to finance his habit. Once "exposed," the Bar fired him—but had Betty deliver the message.

Pot, Coke, and Dubious Staff Members

Ann Arbor tolerated pot use more than most cities. It was out in the open. Cocaine, however, was everybody's expensive little secret. During the early seventies its use in the Del Rio community was on the rise. The police were not about to treat its presence as lightly as they did pot.

In July, the following notice was tacked up on the Del Rio bulletin board:

Owners' Statement—A Hard Line on Hard Drugs

Hard drugs are illegal. Usage or sale of cocaine, etc. is punishable by jail. It is a felony. Twenty-four persons were arrested in Ann Arbor this spring on charges of dealing cocaine, etc.

Because the state has vested in us, the owners, the authority to sell liquor, it also requires that we uphold the law in the bar. The Del Rio license can be permanently taken away if we, as owners, were to support the use of hard drugs on the premises, in any way.

We, as owners, as lovers of the Del Rio and its license, will not engage in any activities which would circumvent the laws regarding drugs on premises.

Therefore if we, as owners, learn of anyone dealing or using hard drugs on the premises of the Del Rio, we must check into the actions of that person. If the charges are true, the person will be dropped from the payroll or 86'd if a customer.

There is no other position that the owners can take on this issue.

The Del Rio has had the policy of no drugs on the premises since its opening. There is no way it is possible in the eyes of the law and the police to have any other policy. The Sunday Meeting reaffirmed this understanding.

Just as we all uphold the 2:30 a.m. closing hour, then none of us have any choice on this issue in the eyes of the law while on the premises of the Del Rio Bar.

Ernie Harburg
Rick Burgess
Torry Harburg

There was quite a buzz among the workers after everyone had read the "proclamation." Those who never touched cocaine laughed it off as necessary paranoia to appease the police community. Some who occasionally used the powdery drug vowed to be more discreet and less obvious about it. But the person whose coke use was the most blatant (and one of the main reasons for the posting of the statement) laughed it off.

Jack the bartender had been at the Del Rio since the beginning and felt immune to such edicts from the "so-called owners." Surely I'm not worried, he thought. Hey, I'm one of the original Del Rio family members. Jack had another reason for feeling safe. He was very generous with his coke, always *willing to share it with whoever was in his circle of friends and co-workers. It wasn't until later that summer that the reason for his generosity came to light.*

It started when the following notice was posted on the bulletin board:

Employees—

It has been rumored that among Del Rio employees are those who are covertly ripping off the bar by pocketing money from customers which should have gone for paying their tabs. All of us take liberties with the system, but this type of abuse greatly exceeds proper standards of behavior.

If the rumors are true, then we as employees must recognize the problem and come to grips with it. Also, we still have a problem in that particular names are associated with the rumors. I feel, along with others, that this subject should be part of the next staff meeting and that it be dealt with in a rational manner. There should be no witch hunts and no mud slinging. If we have a problem, let's deal with it. If we don't, let's end the rumors now!

We also might want to discuss our honor-based system in general.

This notice is not written in any spirit of self-righteousness or malice. No vigilante group or "moles" are involved. Personally, I don't feel that I'm any more moral than anyone else. However, I (and probably most of us) like working in a system based on the honor of the employee without some bureaucratic structure keeping tabs on everything we do. And we don't want it to change either because of the abuse mentioned above or because of the rumor mill.

—Elvin and other concerned Del Rio employees

If some thought the hard drug warning was a hoot, they were certainly more seriously disturbed about anyone in the Del Rio family ripping off our business.

Jack showed no concern about this new posting. In his head it wasn't like he was actually stealing when he took the money. He was just redistributing the wealth, buying coke, and returning part of it to some of his co-workers. And because Jack was smooth, no one had ever caught him actually stealing money. Except Rick.

Rick had seen Jack pocket money that should have gone into the register, but Rick didn't like confrontations. He had talked to only Ernie and Torry about it. One day a long-time regular, who spent hours each day sitting at the end of the bar, had also watched Jack pocket money repeatedly. He mentioned it to Rick and Ernie, so they had further proof. However, they were "owners" and whenever they brought up having problems with Jack, the staff wrote it off as personality conflicts. Jack was staff and to many workers, staff had to stick together against the "establishment owners." And some of this staff was being supplied with free nose-candy by their friend Jack.

Not everyone on the Del Rio staff felt antagonism toward the owners. And some weren't too fond of Jack, either, but had never seen him do anything blatantly wrong. Tina worked with Jack often enough and got along with him all right. She'd heard him talk, but had no proof. Jack continued his blatant behavior and decried the owners for being against him. Then, during one late shift, Tina watched as Jack stuffed a wad of bills in his pocket and threw away the check instead of ringing it up. She freaked.

"What the fuck are you doing?!" she confronted him. The rumors were true. She saw it with her own eyes. Rick and Ernie were telling the truth.

Jack looked hurt. He had no excuse this time, but put on his puppy-dog eyes anyway. He tried to act nonchalant, but Tina had him.

"I can't believe you're ripping us off like that!" she screamed. "You can't do that! You're done!"

Jack had no defense. He just walked out the door. Tina talked to her co-workers about the crisis. Since it was late and not too busy, they decided to close the bar early. Tina called Rick and told him what had happened. He suggested a meeting at his house. Now.

Within half an hour the bar was cleaned up and closed down. A group of seven staff met with Rick, Ernie, and Torry. Many wanted to fire Jack immediately. Others still had trouble believing Jack had done that much damage to the bar's income. But, Tina was totally trustworthy. In the end, the others agreed. If she had seen the rip-off it must have happened. They were shocked to think their profits were disappearing, and especially disheartened to think the money was going to support a coke habit.

Jack was smooth and convincing when it came to protecting his fantasy world. His outer look and manners never revealed what may have been going on inside him. He would deal with this situation using his favored method: denial. He never bothered to do anything after Tina's confrontation. Maybe it would all go away.

It didn't. Accusations had flown at the meeting and landed on the absent bartender. For many of the staff it all came together for the first time. Of course—that's why Jack did this or that. Sure, I saw him do that once. Yeah, I never realized. Hey, I figured he was just really generous, thought one coke user to himself.

It didn't take long to convict Jack, and the sentence was obvious. He could no longer be trusted to work at the Del Rio. Now for the hard part. How do we fire him? Firing an employee was such a rarity and so difficult that there was no easy answer. It was one time the communal business family didn't want to deal with an aspect of running the business. But there was no disagreement about who should do the firing. Let Ernie, the father figure, do it. The workers were happy to act as owners when it came to eating and drinking for free, setting their own schedules, and sharing the profits, but with something this unpleasant, Ernie could be the "boss."

Ernie called Jack and told him about the meeting and said that everyone had agreed that Jack was fired. Jack slammed down the phone.

The next day, Jack, the injured puppy, stormed into the bar and told everyone that Ernie had screamed at him and cursed him and fired him out of hatred. But the real truth had already made the rounds. Everyone knew Jack had been stealing from the bar to buy cocaine. Even those staff members who occasionally used coke or had been given some by "generous" Jack, found his actions uncool and agreed that he should no longer work at the Del Rio.

Jack was finished and none of his smoothness could get him out of this reality. He walked out with his tail between his legs and the Del Rio family felt relieved to be done with him.

Years later, Jack returned, snuck into the bar at night, and stole $2,000 from the basement safe. But he left $2,000 in the safe! Another long story, another Del Rio mystery. The cops called Ernie, Rick, and Betty into the station and then threw them out when they learned that half the staff had keys to the Bar and *all had access to the cash register and a key to the safe!*

Another crisis about firing reported by Larry:

At the next Sunday meeting, Jack's firing was well discussed. People agreed there had to be a fairer way than sending Ernie to do the dirty work. After some discussion it was agreed that for any future firings, one owner and two staff persons would confront the person to be fired. It was only a matter of months before the new system was tested.

Doreen had been a Del Rio waitress for nearly six months, but had never really fit in. She would get depressed and drink too much and neglect her customers. Other staff members would talk to her and try to remind her of the responsibility that each worker had to do their job without supervision. If someone was constantly falling short, it made everyone else's job that much more difficult.

Doreen would seem to improve slightly after these talks, then revert to giving bad service again. Good service was important at the Del Rio. It kept customers coming back. Doreen's service was hurting the Del Rio and it came up as a topic at the next Sunday meeting. She showed up and looked more depressed than usual. People felt sorry for her, which was one reason she had lasted so long without being fired. That and because it still seemed very difficult to fire someone.

When the subject of firing Doreen came up at the meeting, she broke down crying. "No, you can't," she pleaded. "I'll kill myself." (She even threatened to hang herself from a beam in the bar!)

No one wanted to push any further. "We'll talk later," Mary said, trying to calm her, arm around her shoulder. The sobbing subsided and the meeting switched subjects. When the main meeting was over, Ernie, Torry, and Mary (who had her own successful fight with depression) gathered with Doreen in a private meeting. They persuaded Doreen to take a three-week vacation with pay. She'd have a chance to get away from the bar and think about things.

Doreen did have a friend out west whom she'd been wanting to visit, and so agreed that a vacation might be a good idea. She left with the well wishes of her co-workers and three weeks severance pay and smiled with her good-bye hugs.

Two weeks later a postcard arrived at the bar. Doreen was having a wonderful time, her best time in years. She'd met a great guy and was even getting back into her craft work again. Thanks to all, and if it was all right with everyone, she'd like to stay where she was and not come back to the Del Rio.

Everyone was happy for Doreen and relieved that they no longer had to fire her. This time the story had a happy ending.

Consensus at the Del Rio Bar

Perhaps the early Del Rio staff's boldest move was to embrace consensus decision making. Everyone present at the meeting had to agree—or at least not strongly disagree. *The question was* "Does anyone disagree?" *and wait for hands*. No hands, then the discussion was over. Consensus was not new to either Ernie or Torry. At the Institute for Social Research, where Harburg had worked, top people had made decisions by consensus. Ann Arbor Women for Peace, in which Torry had been heavily involved, had embraced consensus. In a 1963 Ann Arbor Women for Peace newsletter, the editors wrote, "Consensus demands a constant working through of diverse opinions until at last a meaningful conclusion has been [reached] at which everyone feels comfortable." With this approach, *one dissenting person could challenge the prevailing idea on the floor, even over several meetings*. Dissent was respected—sometimes with difficulty.

Just how seriously Torry took consensus decision making is reflected in a surviving draft of her writings, showing how she grappled with the concept of meetings in a consensus style of management, which included notes on how to listen, really listen, with respect. She headed one section, "Some Things to Unlearn," and underneath, in outline form, she wrote "(1) Meetings are boring," and (2) "Look. See. Consensus meetings are often live theater: (a) it's unrehearsed, and (b) the ending is unknown."

But the Harburgs and Burgess didn't simply willy-nilly deliver the Bar to the employees. As owners, they participated and, at times, also dissented—for example, when some overzealous staff members at a meeting suggested simply dividing the week's proceeds among themselves. The compromise was that each staff member could eat and drink even when not working. This idea did not last. They also refused to go along with a proposal that would have allowed everyone to work whenever he/she wanted. Finally, the owners refused to sign away one crucial right: to interfere and prevail if it seemed that the Bar was in danger of going under. Ernie Harburg recalled, "I said that the one thing I will not allow is that we go belly-up because of stupid things. I don't mind going under because we didn't get the trade—but for stupid stuff?"

Still, the owners showed themselves most accommodating to the early switch from a traditional management structure. At some point during the late seventies, Torry decided she wanted a salary. Old Del meeting minutes show that this desire proved unpopular among staff members, many of whom regarded her with suspicion just because she was an owner. "If she gets this money," declared one unnamed staff member at a meeting, "Torry should raise her consciousness so it's more in line with the floor workers." The staff did finally vote to give her a salary. Of course, as an owner, Torry could have given herself a salary at any time. But no one was more committed to the vision of an egalitarian workplace than this daughter of a principled labor organizer. Her steadfastness was all the more impressive given that some staff members, as the above comment suggests, were not always very kind to her. Ernie Harburg recalls that she was disturbed when someone on the staff branded her as "bourgeois," a ludicrous label, he said, because Torry, with Betty, were the only ones there at the time who came from a true working-class background. But the Harburgs and Rick Burgess and Betty Vary gamely continued their delegation of power. *It became a hard fact that in the Del Rio Bar no one—not even the owners—could give anyone else an order!* And a customer's "orders" were considered as a collaborative act—part of a giving-to-each-other ceremony.

Ernie Harburg pointed out that historically, consensus decision making has been used successfully by various organizations, such as the Algonquin Federation of the Five Tribes, the Department of Psychology at the University of Michigan, the United Nations Security Council. He said, "The method of solving problems by consensus—not majority voting—allows all group members to provide ideas for the fairest or most equitable resolution of technical or social problems. The solution is perceived by all to be good for the collective—and usually is—and for the individuals." (See "Notes About Consensus" on page 118.)

Still, practically speaking, consensus for the Del meant that many decisions were made slowly—or sometimes by default. But, reflects Betty Vary, "given how strong minded many of the employees were, it's amazing that they could agree as often as they did."

The Recessions

The business cutbacks in the recessions of '71, '81, and, '91 were first met by *voluntary cutbacks of hours by the Bar workers*. In the seventies, the Bar had rejected a "profit-sharing" plan offered by Torry because it was okay to get more money quarterly but not less income if the Bar lost. Finally, the staff wanted and got their regular wages plus an "end-of-year bonus." (Many of the early staff were nonbelievers, and Christmas for many was a negative family ritual.) The major issue of "distributing ownership" was never resolved after it was clear that the Michigan State Liquor Control Commission only permitted a few persons to own a liquor license.

As recessions in the national and local economy occurred in the several cycles, Larry recorded the Del Rio response:

> There is a cycle that happens at the Del Rio as surely as the tides rise and fall. No one notices the high tide when business is good and the money flows. But when it's low and the bar's income slows, everyone pays attention. The usual course is to bring it up at a Sunday meeting, but more often, special meetings are called.
>
> These extra meetings are called the Ad Hoc Finance Committee and they are open to whomever is really concerned about improving bar finances. It is hoped that someone from each group of workers will be at each meeting. Folks get together once a week until the old solutions have been pulled out for recycling and new solutions have been suggested. This is a time when Betty goes over the bar's financial records to give the committee an awareness of problem areas. It's easier to save money when you know where you're losing money.

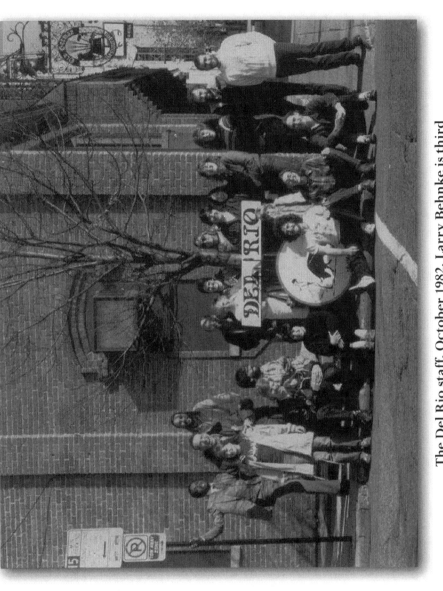

The Del Rio staff, October 1982. Larry Behnke is third from top left, next to Ernie; Rick and Betty are at the left holding the Del Rio sign. *Photo by George Junne.*

The finance meeting on Wednesday afternoon had a good turnout. Betty and Torry were there with the books. Rick and Tommy represented the barts; Lenny and Mary, the waits; and Charlotte as cook. No doortender was present.

"We're having trouble again, folks," said Torry. "It feels like we're in another recession."

Betty drew her finger down a column of figures. "Last month's sales were down. We've got to find ways to cut down on our expenses."

"Time to do the Tighten Up," said Tommy.

"The beer percentage last month was 36 percent!" said Betty. "This is high for us."

"Yeah, this is the area where a bar like ours is supposed to make money," said Torry. "The ideal would be that we pay around 20 percent for draft beer, and make our best profit. That's not been happening."

"The weather's warmed up and we're drinking more," said Lenny.

"Someone is," said Betty. "According to these figures, we're drinking one whole keg of beer a day ourselves."

"Oh, I think we're getting a little help from our friends," said Mary.

"Maybe we need to stop giving our friends free drinks," said Charlotte.

"And never give away food," Tommy added.

Cut out freebies. That was a common suggestion at these meetings. Everyone appeared to agree, and then in a day or two a friend would come in and get a beer on the house or maybe a little bowl of chips. It was hard to remember these meeting plans when you were partying in the Del Rio living room with a good friend or lover.

"We could advertise a little," suggested Mary.

"Hsss!" Tommy threw up his arms and made a cross with his fingers to ward off the dreaded A word. For many Del Rio purists, advertising was a naughty word, something practiced by the establishment. The Del Rio was too cool for that.

"No, really, maybe just some flyers around the neighborhood," protested Mary, "or a little ad in the Sun. What would that hurt?"

"I don't know; we've never done that." Rick shook his head.

"I'm glad that attitude never stopped you from trying sex," Tommy poked at Rick.

Torry brought up another sacred cow: "What about charging a cover for Sunday jazz?"

Rick just shook his head. Sunday jazz was his baby and keeping it free for the masses was cool. Some things are just more important than money. The look on Rick's face spoke volumes. No one bothered to belabor the suggestion.

"Never accept checks!"

"We've got a pile of bounced checks."

"We don't accept checks. See that sign over the register: Sorry—No Checks."

"Friends bounce more checks."

"We're not a bank."

"I never take checks."

"What do you do if a customer doesn't have cash and all they have is a check?"

"OK, what about this," said Torry. "If you must take a check, write your name on it and if it bounces, you are responsible for coming up with the cash to cover it."

"Ouch!"

"Yeah, that sounds good."

"OK, then, it's agreed."

"Good luck!"

"If the waits would clear tables right away, we could get customers inside faster," said Char. "Sometimes people get tired of waiting outside and they go to another bar."

"I think we work fast enough," said Mary.

"And the Del Rio is worth waiting for," Lenny gushed.

"Well, I've seen tables sitting empty for ten minutes with people waiting outside," said Char. "I don't think that's fair to the customers or to us if we're hurting for business."

"I agree," said Torry. "Maybe we could pay a little more attention."

"I think we could compromise on this," said Betty. "We really do need to remember how important the customer is."

"Yeah, they're almost as important as the Del Rio staff," joked Lenny.

But, it wasn't that much of a joke.

Some of the new decisions of the finance committee were implemented for a while, some for longer. Most workers attempted the changes. Any improvements helped keep the bar going and that was in everyone's interest.

The next series of finance meetings dealt with what to do with any profit the bar made. Opinions were divided between those who wanted their wages raised and those who wanted to share the profits as a lump-sum check every quarter. After weeks of arguing and debating, there was never a total agreement. But it was close enough to pleasing most, so Torry typed up and posted this notice:

After much discussion, a decision has been reached. There will be no fixed wage increases and leftover monies will not be shared at the end of every quarter.

In brief summary, I hope this latest round has developed some new understandings. First, making money is not the only goal of the Del Rio: fairness to customers and a nonmanagerial lifestyle for staff are both up there with money. The lifestyle has costs that we are assuming to be worth the benefits, such as the idea that we can each "manage" ourselves in order to cooperate and enjoy working with all others in the bar. Each has some piece of the "goodies" associated elsewhere with owners only: Freebies, control over hours and shifts, the right to ask politely for respect from customers, the right to add hours rather than work overly hard, and the opportunity to be in on all bar decisions via meetings.

These meetings produced the first estimate of the costs of this lifestyle we have chosen—between $20,000 and $23,000 a year. This has been tabbed "daily profit sharing." Other costs of not

*having one person running around supervising, come in mainte-
nance, new equipment, a rip-off now and then, and general loose-
ness, for example, giving away food and drinks to friends.*

*This is the way of life that's been worked out since we began.
Deciding on annual money-sharing means that we share leftover
profit as well as the general risks and costs of our lifestyle.*

*It is now the hope that everyone who digs it will begin the
process of coming together for some wholeness and better feelings.*
— *Torry Pedersen Harburg*

*There were some bitter feelings, especially among those who had wanted the
quarterly profit sharing. Those who wanted higher wages were not so pleased. There
were grumblings that Torry had acted too much like an owner in writing out the
finance meetings' decision. They protested that there had been no Bar consensus.*

*Torry took it all in stride. She had learned long ago that it was impos-
sible to please everyone. To her, it was something of a miracle that such an
organization as the Del Rio could even exist. Other times it took so much
work on her part that she may have been sorry it did exist. Still, in many
ways, it was a satisfying creation.*

Conflicts in the House

There were deep conflicts at times between the goal of an "open" society
and factions in the Bar. In the late seventies, the Bar discovered the majority of cooks were lesbians or "liberated" and did not want to hire men. At
the hiring meeting Rosie, then one of the informal Del leaders (who later
became a lawyer and prosecutor), and Ernie tried to hire a well-qualified
male, Brett Eynon (who was writing antiwar articles contra the University
of Michigan). The cooks refused. They said men smelled. During the
next month the waits, doorts, barts, and a few customers emotionally

"boycotted" the cooks, who finally (tearfully) gave in and hired Brett. It took "eternal vigilance" to maintain an open society at the Del.

As Larry reports, a notice later appeared on the bulletin board:

> *ATTENTION COOKS! Due to the beyond-the-call-of-duty service performed by the cooks for the rest of the Del Rio staff (and all our customers), we out front agree that Cooks Appreciation Week is not only long overdue, but well-deserved. Therefore, we would like you to accept these small gifts as ineffectual, but heartfelt representations of our appreciation.*

Under the proclamation were gift certificates for each of the cooks, redeemable for at least two desserts across the street at Mountain High Ice Cream Parlor. It wasn't money from the register that paid for the gift certificates, but donations from all of the other workers.

Another conflict resolved by consensus took a special five-hour meeting at Rick's house, concerning the issue of wages: should each person get the same wages or should there be a conventional hierarchy of waits (most), barts, cooks, dorts (least)? The hierarchical solution won after a raucous, serious, funny afternoon. The owners weren't mentioned; but they kept their "take" to 10 percent of the gross (there was no net)—a little more than a well-paid wait, whose real income was largely from untaxed tips. This was before the Reagan Republicans lowered taxes for the wealthy and secretly started new taxes for low-income workers like waitpersons. The collective was continually groping, trying out new ways to live by democratic ideals or values like "equality," "fairness," "community," the Golden Rules, peaceable solutions to real problems through consensus.

Another idea that developed involved switching jobs. If newcomers who disliked their job wanted to switch to another one, it was ruled that they would first have to get an okay from their group and from the next group, and then get trained. This encouraged backup people and helped the Bar. Indeed, they even hired the Harburg boys—Tom, a wait; John, a bart; and Mike, a cook.

L–R: Mike, John, Tom, and Ernie Harburg in the seventies; picture taken by Torry.

Problems arose. Sometimes the new group didn't want the new trainee, so discussions ensued. The idea was to train everyone in other jobs, but in fact nobody except Tracy or Suzanne (who created the Del Rio logos and grew to be a fine artist and graphic designer) were capable of learning all the jobs on the floor. "From each according to their abilities, etc." didn't work easily. An attempt was made to write up the Guidelines—at first filling only one page, these rules grew to over fifteen pages—so that problem was never solved.

Another chronic problem was the cooks' wages:

Ellen's hand shot up. "Cooks are working really hard," she said, "now that we're busier. Waits are making more money while we're busting our asses. I think cooks should get a raise."

"But, we've always raised wages for the whole bar," said Tommy, "not just for one group."

"There weren't any cooks at the finance meeting," said Barb, "so how can you ask for more money when you don't know what the total financial picture is?"

Torry spoke. "This year we borrowed $6,000 for renovations. We don't always make profits, but we always have these bills to pay. Then we needed a new ice machine."

"Food isn't a great moneymaker," said Tina. "It's more of a service."

"But having food is good for business," said Ellen, "and we do the managerial tasks so the bar doesn't have that cost."

"But we all do that," said Tommy.

"Just for information," said Torry, "here are our present wages: Cooks get $3.40 an hour, Doortenders get $2.90, Bartenders get $3.00 plus tips, and Waits get $1.90 plus tips, which is at least $5.00 an hour."

Ellen's voice rose. "We're saying that cooks should get $4.00 an hour. Getting less is making us feel really uncomfortable."

"Yeah," said Ed. "There may not be enough profit to do everything we want, but cooks are putting in more work than they're getting paid for."

Ernie had been quiet, but it was time for him to toss in one of his radical gems, "Philosophically, I think everyone should get the same hourly wage!"

Groans. Hoots. "No!" "Then we'd have to rotate jobs!" "But, this isn't a true cooperative." "What is it?" "It's this."

Ernie chuckled. "OK, we have just so much profit; what are we going to do with it? If the cooks want it all, what does the rest of the bar have to say?"

"We deserve more," said Ellen. "Cooks are stuck back there in the kitchen with no feedback."

"Well, you're getting it now," said Mary. "You're saying you want money commensurate with your work. Then when business goes down, are you willing to cut back your pay?"

Back and forth it went, the same and different arguments until the workers tired and the words passed them by. Then Ellen woke everyone up.

"We're really uncomfortable," Ellen said loudly. "We want clear negotiations by Wednesday or we're prepared to walk out. We feel bad about doing this, but we're desperate!"

"WHAT?!"

"What was that statement?" asked Tommy in disbelief.

Ernie spoke: "The cooks are going to quit if they don't get a raise."

"That's strong-arming," said Barb. "My opinion is FUCK YOU!"

"Yeah," said Pete. "I don't think I like working with people who 'cooperate' like that."

"Would the cooks be willing to wait until Monday?" said Mary.

"For the ultimatum?" said Ernie.

"Wait, let's work this out," said Mary. "Although I don't think anyone should get a raise until fall."

"We've been through this before," said Ernie. "No one is going to be coerced. If you want to negotiate the way this bar has always done, we will. Otherwise, go ahead and walk out."

Torry threw in her clinker: "You can always hire a manager."

"NO!"

"Well, you owners always . . . " started Ellen.

"Wait!" said Ernie. "You're putting the 'owners' in a conventional manager-worker situation, but we're trying to do something different here."

"Well, do we have a master plan for a long-range ideal?" said Ellen. "Like, profit sharing is a bullshit phrase. It's lukewarm. The Del Rio experiment is . . . half capitalist, half socialist. It's . . . I don't know."

"We don't always know either," said Torry. "That's why we get together and try to work it out."

The discussion dwindled and people were getting burned out. There was still a strong feeling to resolve the differences, however. Mary suggested a meeting with Betty the next afternoon for anyone who was willing to take a detailed look at the books. She urged all cooks to attend. Betty said that'd be fine with her.

A formula for annual "profit distribution" was finally worked out based on "hours worked," largely conceived and led to consensus by Betty's patience.[42] Betty was the true ombuds person in the Del Rio community.

A quiet afternoon at the Del

Also in the Seventies

In the seventies, it was also agreed that any customer or vendor with a grievance could talk to the collective at the monthly meeting—which led to several dramatic confrontations as the Del was accused at different times of being racist, sexist (against men), greedy (prices too high), and arrogant. In each case the aggrieved customer, most of whom had been 86'd (banned) from the bar, appeared at the monthly meeting and discussed the issue in front of the group with the Delroids involved. All of the customers went away somewhat assuaged *but the group heard their charges loud and clear!* In one encounter, Big John (the nickname of a very large customer recently released from a mental hospital) was allowed to keep coming to the Bar if he signed a contract to keep taking his pills; his good behavior lasted for several months until he broke the contract and was reluctantly 86'd at the Sunday meeting. Another person who left the Del bewildered was the union organizer from Detroit. He spent only one day learning how the staff did not need a union to get what they wanted—the union didn't supply food and good times, etc., etc. He finally got tipsy from all the free liquor and left at the Midnight Tequila time—never to return.

While the Del Rio staff was discovering how to function as a collective, the Bar continued to flourish. Former bartender Paul Gogo (who so loved the place he gave out cards that read "Mr. Del Rio") recalls that in the years he worked, 1972 to 1978, "it [the Bar] was full—always full! You had to throw them out at two o'clock." The Sunday jazz sessions presented some of Detroit's top talent, attracting customers from all over greater Detroit.

The Del itself underwent a facelift in the mid-seventies. Its sandstone facade was replaced by a design Rick and Ernie found in Montreal; later, in the mid-eighties, the side windows were replaced by stained glass. Suddenly, the Bar, though still dark by most standards, was a good deal brighter. Before the renovation, it was so dark that a few couples were occasionally found *in flagrante* in the dark corners on the floor

GOING TO RIO
by Julie Hinds
Ann Arbor News (supplement), November 19, 1982

1969—Those were the good old days. Where have all the radicals gone? Where is that tough, cocky attitude? Where are the real places to drink beer?

1982—we're drowning in a sea of pink and green as students try to out-conform each other. We sup our beer at Charley's or Dooley's, where happy, preppy, peppy plasticity is the order of the day.

That's o.k.—if you're good at that sort of thing. But if you long for a time when the hair was longer, the clothes more rumpled, and the drunken statements more profound, there's still an oasis on the Ann Arbor bar circuit. This haven of authenticity? Del Rio.

Located at 122 W. Washington, this comfortable bar with foodstuffs is frozen in a time when Ann Arbor was more, well, mellow. Bizarre modes of dress and thought are not only accepted here, they're encouraged. The waiters, with their ponytails . . . prepackaged top-40 tunes here like the swinging bars serve up—the music is blues, jazz, rock, loud.

Sure, the physical setting leaves something to be desired. Although it's located next to some of the nicest restaurants in town—the Earle, Old German—the neighborhood is definitely seedy. Far away from the shiny student sanctums, it's not really a place to stroll at night without a big friend or a big dog.

Inside, however, the atmosphere is dark, woody, and intimate. The capacity is small—about 50 people [actually 70]—and encourages thoughtful conversation. A fabulously ornate ceiling floats overhead. And when the closing lights go on, the red lamps merely flicker a tad brighter—almost as if the bar is sorry to see its patrons go home.

On a typical night, the crowd is predominantly townies, with a few graduate students and a mere sprinkling of undergrads. No freshmen (without savvy) allowed—IDs are strictly checked at the door.

The prices run from convenient to damn cheap. Del Rio knows that if you're slightly counterculture, you probably don't have a lot of money. For hard-core poverty cases, the plain, but filling, burrito is a mere 85 cents. The $1.95 deluxe burrito can easily feed two. Other staples on the menu are pizza, nachos, and the beer-steamed Detburger (created, according to the menu, by J. Detwiler, jazz musician and former bartender).

The menu is as mysterious as some of the customers. Two hard boiled eggs for 40 cents, bread and butter for 35 cents. Who orders these items? Anorexics? And who put the fish tank on top of the cigarette machine? Answers to these questions need not be sought. They add to the place's mystique.

The Complete bar offers Stroh's signature, Stroh's dark, O'Keefe Ale, and Heineken on tap. A pitcher runs from $4.50 to $6.75. The dark beer's the best for blending with the atmosphere.

It's fun being a student. But it's a tough image to keep up. Just think of all those Shetlands and Oxfords you have to keep clean. When looking nice and acting nice and going out to a nice place is just too much to bear, let your hair down and go to Del Rio. Real people are welcome.

Neighborhood

The improvement in the Del's immediate neighborhood helped, too. The Del Rio owners, mostly Torry, founded and were active in a neighborhood association of local businesses determined to improve their surroundings. Torry Harburg published a newsletter for the West Side Neighborhood

Group, promoting efforts such as the paving of a public alley, the addition of new streetlights, and, less tangibly, goodwill among the merchants. This newsletter led to the start-up of the *Ann Arbor Observer* through the efforts of Mary Hunt, whom Torry had hired. Eventually, other businesses—a used bookstore, an art gallery—opened nearby, and the West Side neighborhood began to attract pedestrians. After the Harburgs and Rick Burgess purchased the to-be-abandoned Hotel Earle across the street, they opened the popular Earle Restaurant in 1978—a "straighter" and more gourmet venue for suit-and-skirt professionals—which is still (2008) running and where Burgess played and led his jazz group.

The Burrito Team

Larry writes:

> *The Del Rio was serving fewer burgers these days because of a new menu item. When Lenny returned from his trip to California, he reported on a new popular food out there: burritos. He thought burritos would be perfect for a bar named Del Rio. They would be a good protein alternative to burgers, they'd be cheap, easy to make, and no one else in Ann Arbor was serving them. Lenny looked into supplies and costs and made up samples. He brought his proposal to a Sunday meeting and everyone agreed to give them a try. They were a hit. Within two years, one-quarter of all the food sold at the Del Rio was burritos. That was a three-way tie with burgers and salads.*

Artwork by Larry Behnke

Just so the servers will know, the cook writes the Soup of the Day on a posted list. For feedback to the cooks, servers write comments on each day's soup, most often real and sometimes silly:

Soup of the Day	Comments
Navy Bean......................	Hey, man, it's a gas.
Cream of Leach.................	Really sucks.
Integrated Soup: White Bean and Black Olive.................	Some people wouldn't eat it, but liked it if they tried it.
Lima Bean......................	It sells better if you call it Butter Bean with Veggies
Cream of Spinach...............	Who'd a thunk spinach could taste this good
Leek..............................	Another name for urine (piss poor)
Gazpacho........................	Excellent, but make it on a hot day, not a cold, rainy one
Sweet Potato (tomato base).....	Easily one of the definitive sweet potato soups. It confused my taste buds.
Lentil Veggie....................	It left me yearning for dark encounters and secret, gaping wizardoolies
Potato Garlic....................	Too much garlic—not sociable. Not enough garlic.
Jean's Veggie Bean..............	What would Brando do? Probably fart and grin.
Borscht...........................	Hey, it's good (true confessions of a beet hater)
Mushroom with Onion..........	You did something right!
Aunt Kate's Corn Chowder.....	My favorite soup in weeks
Ron's Tater Soop.................	Reasonably delightful, tersely laconic, pithy
Mock Turtle Soup...............	Curdled tahini? Maybe it's mock curdle soup.

Black-eyed Pea....................	Everybody loved it, customers raved, puppy dogs barked
Ed's Cold Cuke Yogurt Soup...	A seasoned veteran says, "More!"
Slightly Creamed Carrot.........	My taste buds had orgasms and cried for more.
Born Again Chocolate Tomato	Blessed.
Corn de la Crème.................	One customer said, "Best soup I've ever had in my life!"
Barley Vegetable.................	Don't be gruel . . . to the one you love.
Vichyssoise.......................	This is the worst soup I ever tasted.
Crème de Fungi.................	Kowabungi!
Mexican Corn.....................	Oh, it's been awhile; good to have you back
Garbanzo.........................	Too many Ceci Beans and not enough Chick Peas
Charlotte's Mushroom...........	Silly Cybin met a pyman for to feed his head.
Cream of Cauliflower............	Ecstatic eating at its best
Mushroom Barley................	Mixed reviews; some loved it, some hated it
Ital Vital Jamaican Soup.........	Strange beautiful majestic dream. Surprisingly good, although cooked bananas go against my cultural up-bringing
Under-the-Influence Soup......	It has a nice aura to it. Tastes good, too.
Cream of Tomato Rice..........	The Sunday staff ate half of it.
Carrot.............................	If you carrot all, you'll like this soup.
Minestrone.......................	Yum-o-rama!
Asparagus Cream.................	So good it never made it to the customers

Mushroom.......................	Good, but light on the 'shrooms— Sinister forces have been selectively hoarding mass quantities of 'shrooms.
Lentil............................	One customer said, "What is this?— Mt. St.Helen's?
Onion............................	Quite delicious, actually. I am small, I am mighty, what am I? I am Onion! Never take liberties with an onion; it will get back at you.
Vegetable Ed....................	Boring! Exciting! It's gone.

—Courtesy of Larry Behnke

In the mid-seventies, the Del narrowly escaped destruction. "On April Fools' Day, Torry called me—I thought she was kidding me—to say the Old German [next door] was on fire and the Del Rio might go next," recalled Vary. Happily, the fire was extinguished in time to spare the Del. Sixteen inches of 1869 brick wall made the difference!

Its escape from demise by fire was just one near miss the Bar enjoyed during its first decade. Ex-employees recall deliciously wild parties, where employees danced on the bar and booze flowed freely. And then there was the barely hidden pot smoking. In retrospect, some ex-employees believe that the police knew about the marijuana violations but were reluctant to intervene. After all, *the violence at the Del Rio Bar was reduced to about zero compared to the prior history of the Del Rio*. Peace was real.

The Del Rio and the City Council

The Del also had its own City Council members! Larry reports:

In Washington, D.C., in the Smithsonian's National Museum of American History is a display case that stands alone. Above the case are the words, "The YouthVote." A quarter of the case holds artifacts of a particular youth vote success story. It holds campaign posters for Jerry DeGrieck and Nancy Wechsler. Another poster advertises a fund-raising dance for their political group, the Human Rights Party. Next to it is the front page of the Detroit Free Press with its lead story telling about the victory of Jerry and Nancy in the race for Ann Arbor City Council. A successful coalition of college students and counterculture hippies elected them to a position of real power in the city government.

When the Del Rio needed a new waitperson a hiring meeting was held and Jerry showed up. This was after the April 1972 city election. Jerry was thrilled to be a new councilman, but the position didn't pay the rent. In fact it didn't pay any money at all. He desperately needed a job and he thought it would be fine and fun to work at the Del Rio Bar.

At the hiring meeting Jerry made an impassioned plea to be hired. When the applicants left and the staff had their discussions, there was some concern that Jerry would be too political in a bar where an attempt was made to embrace all kinds of people. Others argued that the Del Rio was already making a political statement just by the way it was run. In the end it was a matter of Jerry being likeable and having the necessary waiting skills for the job. A consensus was reached and he was hired.

Lenny had been the only male waitperson and wasn't too sure about Jerry until he got to know him. He found in Jerry similar values and that flame of passionate power of the people that burned in many of Ann Arbor's youth during that magical year. Lenny never had a complaint about Jerry DeGrieck. Jerry did his job well and was eager to please. His face held a perpetual grin.

Jerry had been on the student council while attending the University of Michigan. He was the student body vice president. His political leanings were toward the left. He was definitely against the war in Vietnam.

Nancy Wechsler wasn't as cheerful as Jerry, but she too, was concerned about youth struggles and equality for all. She could be called a feminist of those early times when women were casting off the roles that men had for so long defined for them. She was more serious than Jerry and held anger toward any injustices done to her community of peers.

Both Nancy and Jerry were dissatisfied with the politics of Ann Arbor city government. They had a feeling that if enough of their equally dissatis-fied peers could be persuaded to vote in that city election, then they might have a chance of winning. They drew some of their support from liberal Democrats, but much of it came from the countercultural community repre-sented by the Rainbow People's Party.

The RPP knew it didn't have much chance of winning a seat on the city council with their platform of "Rock'n'Roll, Dope, and Fucking in the Streets." Still, one of their members, Genie Plamondon, gave it a try. She had to run in a ward that was mostly Republican and she didn't have a chance. The RPP knew it would be more effective to back Nancy and Jerry, who were running in wards that housed mostly students and Democrats. The RPP contributed their knowl-edge of fundraising musical events and got poster artist Gary Grimshaw to do flyers. They devoted many Ann Arbor Sun articles to the election and helped get voters registered. If Nancy and Jerry won, so did the Rainbow People's Party.

The election victory by the Human Rights Party candidates shocked the straight community, which had dismissed the vocal mass of rowdy kids. The election results were significant enough to receive national news cov-erage, and a place in history at the Smithsonian. But the real benefits of Nancy and Jerry's city council seats were only beginning. None of the three parties held a majority on the council. The Human Rights Party platform was much closer to the Democrats than to the Republicans. When the liberal Democrats on the council united with Nancy and Jerry, they had a majority of power over the Republicans. When they worked together they made magic things happen for the student / hippie / youth culture of Ann Arbor.

A revenue-sharing ordinance was created to make money available for liberal endeavors. Some of the city's money was used for free rock concerts held every Sunday afternoon in the huge field next to Huron High School. Other money was used for the People's Ballroom, for crisis counseling at the Ozone House, for the Drug Help Clinic, for free legal aid, and for the Free People's Clinic. A Human Rights Ordinance was passed to assure fairness for all minority groups. A tenants' rights group was able to get a rent control referendum put on the ballot.

The most radical change made by the new city power structure was that it reduced the pot penalty. From now on, possession, use, and sale of marijuana in Ann Arbor would be "punished" by a $5 fine. If and when a policeman decided to enforce the new city law, he issued the fine in the form of a $5 "parking ticket" to be taken to city hall for payment. Some people tried to get caught for the novelty of it all, but in most cases it was easier for police to ignore the pot smokers. It would have cost the city more to process the fine and ticket than the $5 it brought in.

The golden age of Ann Arbor's counterculture flourished during Nancy and Jerry's term in office. They were serious about their duties but weren't above riling the Republicans for the hell of it. The Del Rio Bar was their office for meeting colleagues and working out policies. It was a nonthreatening, like-minded place to hang out and party.

Nancy Wechsler and Jerry DeGrieck had one other surprise for the straight community, which they waited until after they'd won the election to reveal. It turned out that they were both gay.

Jerry was comfortable with being gay, but not with admitting it. It was only after he'd worked at the Del Rio a while, after he'd been "adopted" by this new family, that he felt it would be okay to come out. Late night, after-work talks with his co-workers convinced Jerry that he had a secure place in the community.

The nurturing atmosphere of the bar family peaked for Jerry at the summer Del Rio picnic. Sitting on a blanket near the lake in the park, surrounded by friends, eating, drinking, and joking all brought Jerry to the realization that he was accepted here, no matter what his sexual orientation. Once he talked about it, it didn't seem like that big a deal. The nurturing bar folk accepted his gayness the way they'd already accepted Jerry.

Nancy came out around the same time. Some members of the Human Rights Party thought Jerry and Nancy "flaunted their gayness" for political reasons, but it really was more related to having found the most comfortable time to admit it. Their work was never affected by it and in the eyes of their consultants, they brought many fine improvements to the city of Ann Arbor.

Post-Seventies and Reagan

The Del Rio's first decade ended somberly with Torry Pedersen Harburg's death in 1981. Ernie's father also died that year and the Bar people supported him with love. Earlier that year, two other employees had died— one while parachuting, the other in a freak fire in Algeria. As employee Gail Grigsby (1975–85) recalled, the losses shook up the young staff, who were also hearing for the first time about a disease called AIDS. "We were forced to grow up a little bit," said Grigsby. The Vietnam War had finally ended. The start of the conservative Reagan years, combined with increasing concerns about the Bar's liability began a new, somewhat less buoyant era for the Bar and for the Reagan-led nation.

As the tumultuous sixties and seventies receded into history, Ann Arbor's countercultural scene gradually faded, and institutions associated with the bakeries, coffeehouses, a beloved vegetarian restaurant, the underground newspaper, the *Sun*—became scarce or disappeared. The local downtown restaurant and bar scene grew, with most of the newcomers part of a national chain. But the Del—defiantly true to its unconventional underpinnings—stayed open, holding a sort of monopoly on the glory days.

HANGING OUT AT THE DEL
by Laura McReynolds
Ann Arbor News (Restaurant Review, May 1994)

The Del Rio is more than a bar, it's a way of life. Witness my friends and longtime Del Rio loyalists Kevin and Marge, who not only got married at the Del Rio, they also enlisted one of the bartenders to perform the ceremony.

"We had about three days left before our marriage license expired," Marge remembers. At the last minute, they discovered that one of the Del Rio bartenders also happened to be a mail order minister of the Church of Universal Life. They were married there that very day, complete with ad-libbed wedding vows, cheering customers, and a rose bought for them by a couple who had themselves met at the Del.

Marge and Kevin are just two of a large, continually evolving group of Del Rio regulars, an irreverent, bohemian mix of artists, poets, musicians and working folk who don't simply frequent the place, they help define it. For that matter, the very fact that they hang out there says something about them. This isn't just a place they go, it's a part of who they are.

The Del inspires unusually strong feelings on the other side of the bar, too. One of the reasons is its unique cooperative management structure. The bar is owned by local musician Rick Burgess and entrepreneur Ernie Harburg [by this time, Betty Vary was also a part-time owner from shares gifted to her by Torry and Ernie's three sons], but it's run by its cooks, bartenders, waitstaff and doortenders, each of whom get a share of the profits and have an equal say in how it operates.

The Del turned 25 last Friday, but its décor has remained pretty much the same over the years. It's dramatically dim and funky by night, when the black tin ceiling and rotating artwork is lit by candles in nubbly amber glass, the shimmering fish tank behind the bar, and heavy red lanterns overhead. *During the day, it can be almost heartbreakingly beautiful, especially at dusk when the setting sun filters in through the leaded glass windows and casts the Del's brick and rough planked walls in a golden, nostalgic light.*

A significant part of the Del Rio's distinctive atmosphere is its music, an eclectic collection dubbed onto more than 1200 cassettes and played, sometimes crashingly loud, by the bartender on duty. Don't bother making requests or asking them to turn it down. Since the customers—and for that matter, many of the staff—can't agree on genre or volume, the employees have voted to give the bartenders complete autonomy.

The Del's menu hasn't changed much, either. Everything's made from impeccably fresh ingredients in-house, from imaginative soups such as Hungarian mushroom and a spicy, pungent carrot-ginger to the amazing cheesecakes baked by cook Nancy in inventive flavors such as apricot amaretto.

It's an idiosyncratic marriage of old-fashioned bar standards and vegetarian cuisine, with hard-boiled eggs, peanuts and burgers co-existing quite happily alongside soy cheese, beans with rice and the Del's moist, nutty-tasting tempeh burger served on a sweet, soft whole wheat bun. There's a decided emphasis on Tex-Mex: tostadas, quesadillas and the popular, thoroughly respectable burritos, packed tight with beans and cheese and moistened with a mild taco sauce.

Don't let all the veggie stuff fool you, though; the Del Rio's trademark Detburger is one of the best—and certainly the most interesting—cheeseburgers in town. It's top quality Knight's beef topped with a delicious heady mélange of mushrooms, green pepper, black olives and onion steamed in beer. Order it rare if you like, but the patty's a little thin and the grill is very hot. I've never seen one come out anything but medium.

I love the pizza here, but the crunchy, strongly flavored whole wheat crust is an acquired taste. You can get a whole or half pie topped with beef or pepperoni, but I think the dough's underlying sweetness works best with vegetables. I highly recommend feta, onion, green pepper and jalapeno.

The vegetable stir-fry is new on the menu, and it's a winner. It's a happy, fresh-tasting jumble of mushrooms, green peppers, onions and seasonal vegetables brightened by a light ginger sesame sauce and served over rice. Add tofu or tempeh for an extra buck.

The Del has a reputation for insularity and terrible service, but in recent visits I haven't seen any real evidence of either. I will say that more than most bars, the Del Rio is probably not for everybody. And I'm willing to bet that that's the way they like it.

Note to those who've been wondering: Yes, the Mrs. Butterworth's next to the monk-shaped Frangelico bottle behind the bar is there as a joke. Order a shot at your own risk. "If you order it," laughs bartender and cook Janet Ledworth, "we'll make you drink it."

The Delroids: Twenty-fifth Reunion

On the afternoon of June 18, 1995, more than 200 former Del Rio employees from around the nation and quite a few customers gathered together at a nearby park to celebrate the Bar's twenty-fifth anniversary. For an afternoon, the participants, some of whom still sported long hair and hippie-style clothes, played badminton, threw Frisbees, and showed off children and babies to former co-workers they hadn't seen for years. It had not been that difficult for Vary to find most of them, because they'd either stayed in touch with the Del or with other ex-employees whom Vary knew. To many of the Del employees, the lasting friendships they made were the Bar's biggest legacy. "More than the people I keep in touch with from high school, friends from college, from graduate school," says Steve Auerbach, he has stayed close to his friends from the Del Rio.

The late eighties: Still in casual dress in spite of the new conservative years. Ernie is at the extreme right, Rick is third from right and Betty is the white-haired lady in the center.

The Delroids also made comments:

Lenny wasn't always content living life; he also found it fun to analyze it. To Lenny, the Del Rio was a social phenomenon that he'd watched grow and change and remain endlessly fascinating. He'd cooked, doortended, bartended, and waited tables. He'd attended most of the general meetings, learned the processes, and heard much talk about what made the Del Rio special. Still, he continued in his quest to try to define what it is.

What the Del Means to Me

One day Lenny tacked up a large sheet of paper to the bulletin board. On the top in bold psychedelic lettering, he wrote:

"WHAT THE DEL MEANS TO ME."

After less than a week the paper was full of scrawled impressions, jokes:

"A nice corner bar that suffers from delusions of grandeur."

"A place of employment which tries to be a community and sometimes succeeds, and which tries to serve the community and sometimes succeeds."

"A fine institution with nice innkeepers."

"A place where you get paid to have fun, where you can be crazy without being committed, and where customers and employees are more important than money."

"The stream itself is off the shelf, Del Rio is its name.

A family style that does beguile each kid who ever came

Through that front door of prismic lore; the River flows through all,

And all flow through the River too—it's really quite a ball."

"It's my substitute home where people are nice to me."

"The Del Rio means a million things to me which I refuse to limit to the narrowness of words and the confines of space."

"It's a place where you can listen to nice music and get a good salad and a hot bowl of soup, all for under $2.00."

"The Del Rio is Benevolent Despotism."

"It's an atmosphere created by a staff which moves in musically cooperating rhythm to create a climate of fancy fun."

"Casual. That's what the Del Rio is. Casual."

There's an Art to This Bar
from the *Ann Arbor Observer*

Bars are for booze and art galleries are for culture, right? Not necessarily. There's a friendly neighborhood-type bar in Ann Arbor called the Del Rio that features terrific burgers *and* terrific photography. They use their rustic brick walls to display quality art in various media by Detroit and Ann Arbor artists. Some have shown in other galleries and many are just getting started, but all of them are good.

The exhibits are an extension of the Ann Arbor Museum, the brainchild of Del Rio waitress Josie Rock. Three years ago she decided restaurants, not galleries, were the place to bring art to the people. Today she coordinates shows at the Del Rio, Turtle Island Restaurant, and Eden's Deli, all in Ann Arbor. Shows last three weeks and all works are for sale.

The Del Rio's Detburger is a work of art, too. Smothered in cheese, onions and black olives and basted with beer, it was rated by the *Washington Post* last year as one of the country's top 20 burgers.

Vary, Harburg, and Burgess credit the spirit and drive of the Bar to *unofficial, informal leaders* who rose in each generation of employees. The new leaders brought forth ideas and innovations. The menu was re-created to include burritos and nachos. In 1980, Del Rio employees conceived of decorating the walls in a monthly turnover with photographs and paintings done by local artists. Later, in the nineties, they started and ran an open, free, musical Tuesday night featuring local groups and a monthly "Feed the Poets" reading; local poets got free meals for reading their poems aloud to regular customers.

Charlotte didn't have to work until that evening, but the Del Rio was more than a place to work. It was a cool place to hang out, even for its workers. Char heated her bagel and poured a cup of fresh coffee, then settled into a small table near the back. It was a special time: Poetry Sunday. Char had been writing her own poetry for years and was delighted to think that the Del Rio was now having poetry readings.

Saturday afternoons had been a slow time of the week, until lately. Sam Modica, a likable poet from Texas, had been hanging around the Del Rio, making friends, and thinking about the need for a poetic forum. With its Beatnik origins and atmosphere the Del Rio was perfect. Sam organized the event, printed up flyers, and invited local poets to read. He usually read some of his poetry at the beginning to get things going.

Today's featured poet was a special treat. John Sinclair would be reading some of his work. John was somewhat of a celebrity around Ann Arbor, but not for his poetry. He was a true revolutionary and a hero to many hippies. He was also a thorn in the side of most of the mature population in town, to straight Amerika.

John Sinclair was the Renaissance man of Ann Arbor's counterculture. He had read poetry in Detroit during his beatnik past. He was well versed in blues and jazz and helped organize musical events. He'd published the alternative paper, the Warren-Forrest Sun, which became the Ann Arbor Argus, then the Ann Arbor Sun when Sinclair and friends moved to the more liberal climate of this university town. He musically managed the high energy rock band, the MC5, who created a sound that a decade later would become known as punk rock.

Although Sinclair worked in entertainment, he combined it with political ideology. The thoughts of Chairman Mao surfaced in his political writings. In support of the Black Panther Party, he gathered his white friends who sympathized with blacks and formed the White Panther Party. It later became the Rainbow People's Party to encompass people of all colors.

John Sinclair believed in people controlling their own lives and saw the present power structure as corrupt and self-serving. "Power to the People" was his credo and he worked hard for years to make it a reality. Like the labor organizers of decades past, he sought to organize young people around their unique culture, not for higher wages, but for more creative control in their lives.

Unfortunately the power structure saw him as a threat. A government agent posing as a hippie hounded Sinclair for weeks to get him some pot. Finally, to get the guy off his back, Sinclair gave him two joints and was promptly arrested. Judge Robert J. Columbo, wanting to make an example of this "dangerous" radical, sentenced him to ten years in prison. The effect was not the planned suppression. Rather, now the radical community had a martyr and a cause. "Free John Now" became the rallying cry.

The Ann Arbor Sun printed Sinclair's writings from prison and the youth were exposed to new thoughts and the idea that maybe they really could control their lives. And they weren't afraid to try. Sinclair's imprisonment made the hip community stronger and they united not only to try to get their hero freed but also to implement some of his ideals.

Efforts to get John Sinclair out of jail reached a peak the winter night of a huge concert and rally in Ann Arbor's Crisler Arena. Speakers and musicians sympathetic to the cause donated their talents. Speakers included Rennie Davis, Allen Ginsberg, Jerry Rubin, Ed Sanders, and Bobby Seale. Musicians who showed up to play included Archie Shepp, Phil Ochs, Commander Cody, David Peel, Bob Seger, and Stevie Wonder. (Ernie and Rick got a contact high from sitting in the top balcony!)

Finally John Lennon and Yoko Ono capped the evening with a song they had written for the event, "Ten for Two" (ten years for two joints). The chorus ended with, "We got to, got to, got to set him FREE!"

The political pressure and the popular cultural climate combined to overturn Michigan's harsh marijuana laws. Three days after the Free John concert, the State of Michigan Supreme Court lowered penalties for pot possession from ten years to six months. After twenty-nine months in jail, Sinclair was released along with a hundred other pot prisoners in Michigan. The hip community was ecstatic. The people really did have the power. They were cocksure and giddy about it.

John Sinclair lived with his wife, Leni, and their daughter, Sunny, in a huge former fraternity house on Hill Street. It was known as the Rainbow People's Party commune and housed many of the organizers, newspaper staff artists, and musicians who worked on the people's projects. It was a castle of creative possibilities to many in the youth culture. Through the Ann Arbor Sun articles and RPP house bands, through special events and radio programs, the Rainbow philosophy was spread and gained support among the young and disenchanted. "We're tired of your death culture ways," they said. "You can keep AmeriKa with your genocidal wars. We'll build our own country, Woodstock Nation!" Heady stuff for a bunch of kids just discovering who they were. And helping to lead the way was John Sinclair.

But, today at the Del Rio, John Sinclair had come to read his poetry. He walked through the front door and the people could feel his magnetism. He as a big bear of a man with a bushy beard and wild hair flying out from his head, almost intimidating but for the Santa's twinkle in his eyes. Smiles and greetings and well-wishes met him as he walked up the aisleway. He sat near the makeshift stage and Lenny brought him a beer, on the house, of course.

The Delroids

"The Del Rio has a tendency to hire quirky people who have many interests," said ex-employee Dorothy Dailey, when the Bar was still open. When you meet a Del Rio employee, she went on, "you'll meet an overeducated person with lots of interests." At the reunion, Betty Vary noted that many former Delroids were teachers or lawyers. There were also a female airline pilot, social workers, chefs, small business owners, and, of course, artists, some of whom, like Margaret Parker, the first head cook, settled in Ann Arbor. Apparently very few chose to climb the corporate ladder. A few, like George Junne, a culturally active doortender/bartender, now teaches at the University of Colorado. One media star emerged—Sara Moulton, who now hosts a national TV show on the Food Network. "She was a little dynamo in the kitchen—always testing out food on us," recalled Larry Behnke. "She loved experimenting—we knew she'd go far. We just didn't think it would be on television." The Del was also a place for post-college persons to take the time to experiment with their own career desires— not their parents' or the media's ideas.

For more than thirty years, members of the Del Rio staff met at monthly meetings to vote on issues that ranged from banning a customer to making the place smoke-free (voted down several times). Although the meetings were eventually limited to two hours, they could be exhausting because it took so long to make a decision. "Eventually, you'd get sucked into the minutiae of the Bar," recalled Dorothy Dailey. "Any kind of change in the menu was difficult. Do we add mayonnaise to the sandwich?" The price of a democratic process is at times boredom and fatigue, so it was decided *to limit the monthly meetings to two hours*.

Smoking and the Limits of Consensus

In early 1980 the Del Rio threw out its cigarette machine. But as half of the staff and customers were smokers, the fight to ban smoking raged on as they waited for the City Council to decide the issue, which *never happened*, so the arguments continued.

> *"Next item," Mary raised her voice above everyone talking at once. "A non-smoking section. What about it?"*
>
> *Betty spoke, "The new state law specifies setting aside a table where smoking isn't allowed. How can we comply?"*
>
> *"I think we should have one table where smoking is allowed," said Barb. "This place gets too stinky with smoke."*
>
> *"We need a smoke-eater or two," said Lenny. "We can't breathe."*
>
> *"You got that right," said Tina.*
>
> *"Hold on. We have a lot of customers who smoke." Torry was defensive to the point of being a smokers' rights advocate. She smoked Lark cigarettes*

with the Micronite filter, little granules of charcoal that lulled her into thinking it was safe smoke she was taking deep within her lungs.

"What about the three little tables up front?" suggested Charlotte.

"Yeah, they're sort of off by themselves, anyway," said Lenny.

"Sounds good," said Pete. "What do we need to do?"

"Just remove the ashtrays from those tables," said Betty. "And put a No Smoking Section sign on the wall."

"I don't see why we need three tables," Ernie protested. "The law only calls for one."

"Well, they're so close together," said Char. "If someone smoked at one table it would be smoky at the other two."

"I think we should give nonsmokers that one little section," said Barb.

"I still think one table is enough," said Ernie. In the end he was the only holdout and Ernie was a nonsmoker. (Actually Ernie was in favor of banning all smokers and was trying some reverse psychology.) Perhaps he'd grown tolerant living with a fervent smoker like Torry. He finally gave in and it was agreed to try the nonsmoking section and report any problems at the next general meeting. The air was cleared (a figure of speech) for the next topic.

Consensus doesn't always work on hot issues!

At one typical meeting, in the spring of 2002, the staff spent almost half an hour discussing a customer referred to as "Crutchman." Marco Bruschtein, the group's facilitator, offered a lively description of Crutchman. "He's always sitting at the Bar, making airplane noises. He has a big, huge duffel bag. He's always asking for cigarettes, which isn't allowed. In my opinion," Bruschtein concluded, "he's bad for business, and he has no redeeming qualities." Bruschtein proposed to ban Crutchman from the Bar altogether. Most of the fifteen or so staff members in the room agreed, but one waitress said, "I don't think it's the kind thing to do." There was a lot of back and forth about Crutchman, but when Bruschtein weighed in with the group late in the meeting, the waitress didn't object. Crutchman was

86'd. In the *process of consensus, to withhold open dissent is to agree or grudgingly accept the idea.*

Former employees have reflected on the difference between the Bar and other places they've worked. Mark Grasso recalled that at previous bartending jobs, he was supposed to act as a bouncer—a potentially dangerous job. Here, when a customer proved nasty, all the employees on the floor swarmed around the miscreant until he left. *The rule was "no hands" on any customer.* "It changed the way I thought about things as far as workplace politics hierarchy goes," he said. This nonviolent device for handling customer misbehavior emerged from the early example of Julie Detwiler whose eye-to-eye "moral persuasion" of usually large male customers to cease and desist or leave was a woman's act of skill and courage for an age-old Bar problem.

Vacations with Pay

The paid-vacation policy was simple: After one year, one week; after two years, two weeks; after five years or more, three weeks of paid vacation.

Several scrapbooks of Del Rio memorabilia (old menus, minutes of long-ago meetings, postcards, letters) capture the spirit of Del employees. "Dear Tom," reads a note from a long-ago Del Rio employee. "I am extremely sorry for my snotty little outburst. I beg for your forgiveness. Repentantly yours, Becky."

Other postcards:

> *Dear Folks, Just to let you know I continue to stand for the unhoused, unwashed, etc. Rick, you lied: there's lots of music here, even by your standards. And North Beach is your kind of place. I saw Clifton Chenier on Friday. Now I'm off to a free performance by the San Francisco Mime Troupe in Ho Chi Minh Park.*
>
> *Love, Pete*

Del Rio Crew, Coolin' it in the shade of a mango tree, watching the endless sun on the sea. South America is still in my head, but there are pressures from the police (for one small roach in my pocket!). In Tobago I lived way back in the bush, cooking food (Ital) on a fire, using rainwater, bathing in the river—natural living in the new age we call it. I've been smokin' herb, swimming, dancing the reggae and calypso beat. Ah . . .

Love, Barb

People here are so hospitable. All the magic places are even more intense than I expected. On to Ireland, then Scotland.

Charlotte

Hey y'all! Good karma prevails on this adventure; it is intensely everything from amazing scenery to good people. I've been hiking south through the mountains of North Carolina, the Smokies are still ahead. I've perfected a drawl, but the spit still needs work. Sometimes I wonder what the soup is today at the Del Rio.

Love you! Tina

Things here are crazy as people from all over continue to flock to the end of the rainbow for the holidays. I've met a variety of folks in Key West, but somehow I miss you people and your unique varieties.

Love, Lenny

Dear Del Rio, Two weeks in Paris was either not enough or too much. We've made the trip to the country now, the quaint village of Amborux and our first night were served tΛte de veau—no shit, chopped calf's head. We take the tour tomorrow.

Mary

Gwai-Lo, Hong Kong is a lot like Disneyland. Everyone lives in pagodas and eats live frogs (two tied together!).

Love, Tommy

In Banos, Ecuador we had a huge feast (with your donation) with lovely smiling faces of the poorest of the city. A fine fiesta! Our energy to you.

Barb

DEL RIO
120 West Washington
761-2530

It is unfortunate that the word "mellow" is so overused, because it offers a fitting description for the Del Rio. One of the first renovated eating spots in downtown Ann Arbor, the Del Rio has retained its place as one of the most tasteful. The two large front windows are frame in carved wood. Inside, the bare brick walls host a changing exhibition of paintings and photographs by Ann Arbor artists. Behind the bar is stacked one of the largest tape collections of any local drinking spot. It is dark, softly lit and almost always crowded.

This is a bar patronized by long-time Ann Arbor residents, ex-college students who have chosen to make their home here and professional graduate students. Many of the people you see breakfasting at the Fleetwood Diner appear later in the day at the Del Rio. Dominick's regulars tend to choose this bar for their more serious drinking. Part of its appeal surely lies in the congeniality of the staff. The easy-going but no-nonsense attitude of the crew gives the place a friendlier and more reflective air than its wilder counterparts in town.

The Del Rio is best known, food wise, for the Det Burger, clearly a great hamburger. The pizza at the Del Rio approaches perfection. It comes from the kitchen steaming hot. Even before eating, one can tell this is going to be a winner. It's thicker than most pizzas; the thickness evenly distributed between crust, sauce, cheese and items. The crust is crispy and cooked throughout, a real plus. I found the sauce just a wee bit timid, though it caused no hesitation in my attacking the pie. A great pizza.

Burritos are very tasty and reasonable in price. The Zapata is unbelievable for its price. It's the recommended burrito. Excellent soups are also on the menu. Sunday evenings have informal jazz concerts which are free and well attended.

If you want to discuss Structuralism, Feminism or Marxism or are looking for people to start a new literary magazine, just hang around the Del Rio—you'll find both.

I think of y'all often with warm heart, dark beer, and flashy poetic phrases. Smiles from a distance—touch—feel—dream.

Love, Sam

Dear Folks, Taking a mid-day siesta from the heat, lying underneath the mosquito net in our palm-thatched hut we're renting from a fisherman who gives us fresh fish and keeps us tuned to the Mexican Top 40. . . . Being watched by giant spiders with eyes that glow in the dark.

Love, Charlotte

There's a note written on a menu pad from someone asking for a job: "The Del is the only place I really want to work at. I could work at some corporate place but there would be no reason to dedicate myself to the place." Said Vary, of ex-employees and customers, "Many of them tell us that those days at the Del Rio were the best days of their lives." Their dedication was to the open society and its pleasures of companionship— *liberté*, *egalité*, and *fraternité* and consensus within the dictates of the State Liquor Control Commission.

The Loss of Leadership and the Last Call: 2003

One evening in early December 2003, a handful of people were picketing the Del Rio. Paul Engstrom, a bartender who had worked there eight years, carried a sign that read "Ernie, help! Send the helicopter." The sign referred, of course, to Harburg's welcoming speech, for years delivered to new Del employees at monthly staff meetings. The door opened, and Karen Piehutkoski looked out. Recently married to Rick Burgess, she had also assumed full control over the Del, and her actions—specifically, the sudden firing of a few employees—had precipitated the picketing. "What does your sign mean?" she asked Engstrom. He told her, and she closed the door.

Employees picketing the Del Rio? Shocked longtime customers respected the picket lines—and a couple of them even joined in the protest. At first, the protest appeared successful—business plummeted as though an episode of food poisoning had been reported at the Bar. But the picketing didn't force the owners to negotiate with understandably disgruntled workers and ex-workers. Instead, the owners decided to close the Bar and sell it. New Year's Eve 2003 was the Del's closing night; the evening was part wake and part goodbye party.

What had happened? The Del owners hadn't wanted to close the place, but the national recession in 2001 had, as in past recessions, also hit Ann Arbor. In an interview in 2002, veteran bartender Nick Papalas referred wistfully to the Bar's glory days: "Times have changed around the Del Rio. In the middle of January we used to have people lined up."

Much of the decline had to do with increased competition from newer bars that had sprung up all over the city. Even more mainstream restaurants were competitive. Vary, Burgess, and Harburg felt that the Del couldn't compete successfully without a major shake-up—including a move to traditional management. The Bar's operation as a collective no longer seemed feasible. In years past, a few dedicated employees had always emerged as informal leaders, devoted to maintaining the smooth functioning of the Bar. But over the past decade, this had happened less and less frequently. Most of the *employees of the nineties lacked the idealism of earlier workers* and weren't committed to a collective. To make matters worse, recent employees were almost all part-timers who lacked a big-picture perspective. To the frustration of the owners, some workers took too much advantage of the Bar's 'loose atmosphere to serve free drinks to circles of their friends. This had happened, to be sure, throughout the Del's history, but the problem seemed to be worsening. In the prosperity of the nineties, turnover was high in all the stores and restaurants in Ann Arbor. To counter this, the Del hired more "temps" who were never "acculturated" into the Bar's way of doing business; further, the steady payroll of thirty to forty rose to more than fifty. The Bar collectively was coming apart.

And so were the aging owners, increasingly preoccupied with other concerns, including their health. They all wanted to keep the Bar but to *retire from active management*. Burgess simply stopped coming to the Bar in the early millennium. Vary, still bookkeeper, was the person most involved with day-to-day operations, but after Rick left she cut back, and then announced her retirement. For years, Ernie Harburg had split his time between Ann Arbor and New York, where he lived with his second wife, Deena Rosenberg, and their son, Ben. While still doing his research, he was also busy with the The Yip Harburg Foundation, which he and his sister Marge had set up, to promote both Yip's work and social justice. He was thinking of selling his home in Ann Arbor, which he did after the Bar closed, and became a full-time East Village New Yorker (in a condo four blocks away from where his father was raised 100 years ago!).

For Ernie, the end had come after a Sunday meeting when he had tried to have the full meeting fire a waitperson whose excessive drinking on and off the premises had affected everyone; but he was opposed raucously and she was protected. Ernie deeply believed the Bar must never enable anyone to become alcoholic.

The owners felt it was time for a profound change, So in October 2002, they promoted a hardworking and popular employee to manager, a move that was applauded by the group; but she stepped down after a few months, leaving the bar's governing structure pretty much intact. The owners then went outside the organization for her replacement, but employees resented the new manager from the start. "She, like, married into this giant family who didn't want her there," said former waitress Missy Orge. Disgruntled employees complained of the new manager's lack of restaurant experience. "She asked me how to make a gin and tonic," complained Paul Engstrom.

But the staff's discontent didn't ignite into mutiny until the fall of 2003 when Karen Piehutkoski came on board. Harburg was shocked while explaining, "Rick had suddenly married his half-hippie/half-authoritarian co-vive Piehutkoski and instantly made her a co-owner by giving her power of attorney for his shares." Piehutkoski's appearance coincided with the disappearance of Betty Vary, who sat home, hobbled by an injury. Vary was to spend the last six weeks of the Del Rio's existence glued to the telephone, increasingly agitated, listening to the daily twists and turns of the Del Rio drama as reported by its participants—and the local press.[43]

The longtime owner of Ann Arbor's downtown Kilwin's Chocolate Shoppe, Karen Piehutkoski "came in there just like George Bush or John Wayne, pistols in the holster," said veteran waitress Mary Anne Guidotti. At a staff meeting, Guidotti continued, Piehutkoski bluntly announced that "the Del Rio collective/cooperative is no longer." She then read through a list of "guidelines," adding at the end, "Did I mention 'Work hard'?" Shocked and indignant at this sudden imperiousness, the staff was further infuriated when Piehutkoski posted a memo that read in part: "Failure to represent the Del Rio in a positive way to customers and other employees WILL RESULT IN IMMEDIATE TERMINATION."

Then Piehutkoski began firing people. Mary Anne Guidotti reported as usual for her night shift one evening—and was stunned to learn that she was fired. Incredulous, Guidotti, who had worked at the Del for eight years, demanded an explanation. The only answer she could get from Piehutkoski was "We just don't visualize you as a part of the new Del Rio." Mary Ann began the picketing.

Piehutkoski is straightforward about her role: "My job was to go in and fire." She says that the Bar's increasingly uninvolved owners were reluctant to do the dirty work. Only with a clean sweep of some dyed-in-the-wool employees, the feeling went, could the Bar succeed as a more traditionally run business. But Piehutkoski hadn't reckoned with the fury of employees accustomed to the old Del Rio. "On an emotional level, *they believed that they owned it*," Piehutkoski said. She called her brief involvement with the Del "one of the most painful experiences in my life."

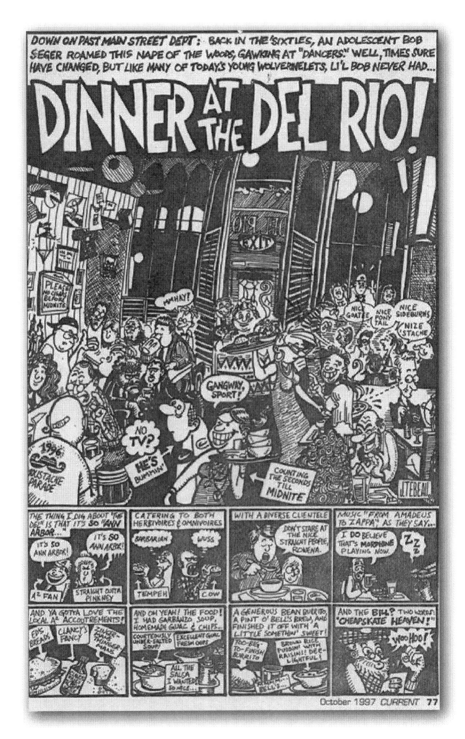

So the final few weeks of the Del were—as its birth, life, and history—marked by turbulence.

A couple of employees met with a representative of the nearby Borders bookstore union (the old Industrial Workers of the World!), and noises were made about unionizing Del workers. The picketing started, and one sign read, "Workers paradise becomes slave pit." Business plunged. Veteran workers detested the new hires, noting contemptuously that one man being groomed for management had worked previously at a chain bar. Then—soon after one angry employee was fired—the Del was vandalized. The Bar counter was slashed, and holes were poked in a restroom wall. Piehutkoski was greatly shaken to find herself the subject of ugly and, she felt, menacing graffiti. A picture resembling her appeared on the restroom wall with a big hole shot through the torso and the warning "No more talk."

The Closing Party: Karen and Rick, front left; Betty standing in rear. Photo by Harveyphotos.com (2004)

Piehutkoski decided she'd had enough. So did the owners. Ultimately, and decisively, Harburg pulled the plug. "We were losing half our income," he said. "The leadership of the Bar was gone. It all went up in smoke." In the words of a well-known song,

The party's over . . .
It's all over . . .
My friend.[44]

The Closing Party

Despite the closing tensions, the New Year's Eve closing party was relaxed. The angry employees absented themselves, as did Ernie, and Betty Vary enjoyed meeting customers and past employees who reminisced fondly about old times. Participants received, as a memento, an original menu of the Bar with an inscription on the back that read, "With love, November 1969–January 2004." At one point a completely naked woman strolled through the Bar, courtesy of a local photographer who sold postcards of nude women shot in local settings. It seemed an appropriate offbeat touch to the closing of the offbeat Bar.

Many mourned the closing. "It was really, really hard to be without the Del Rio, and it still is. I don't think I'm even over it," said Mary Anne Guidotti. Yet there was a sentiment among some that the Bar's 'closing— no matter what the circumstances—was inevitable. It had come into its own in a different era, when Ann Arbor was more politically volatile, more outwardly idealistic, and not so saturated with downtown eateries. The Del had either to be reinvented, or closed. "It outlived its time," said Betty Vary. However, the Harburg family believes that the Del could have survived, but that "there just weren't any leaders to carry out the values. Even the few Delroids who wanted to buy the Bar all finked out!" The real surprise was that the Del Rio had lasted so long. Ex-employee Danny Calderone once marveled, "Somehow it survived. It was amazing how well it survived."

The only "mystery" about the Del Rio according to Harburg was the set of secular, moral rules that governed the conduct of Delroids and were a basic part of the culture but never articulated—unlike Confucius whose guidelines turned into dictates and were somewhat lengthy. But a few of the "underlying mores of Del Rio culture were crudely realized—and this is a personal list," said Harburg:

1. *All persons are born equal and have the basic rights to life, liberty, and the pursuit of happiness.*

2. *Behave toward others as you would have them behave toward you, so be kind and help others.*

3. *Do not do to others what you would not want done to you. So, don't harm others with conduct or speech; keep the wound of truth within reason.*

4. *Don't violate community laws designed to prevent harm or injustice to others, so resist or dissent nonviolently and creatively.*

5. *Feel free to act on the First Amendment and other amendments and continuously innovate others, like term limits for judges, legislatures, and bureaucrats.*[45]

6. *No one has the basic right to order anyone else to do or think or feel*[46] *and never adulate another human being, alive or dead, especially politicians, parents, religious figures, movie / TV stars, and military "heroes."*

7. *Profits should be fairly and proportionately distributed to owners, investors, salaried and wage earners at least annually in all capitalist corporations.*

8. *No leadership should be immune from admitting errors and constantly fixing these errors.*

9. *A valid process of consensus must commit itself to the single law of science: "Do not block the path of inquiry."*[47]

And so forth. Someday even scientists and funders will see the value of systematic study of "secular morality,"[48] *and also how idealisms or visions of a democratic society can be researched and applied.*

Finally, the same child who observed that the emperor had no clothes also noticed about his loving but "married" parents that when love fails, courtesy and consensus must prevail. Or else.

LIGHTS OUT FOR THE NEW DEL RIO, BUT MEMORIES WILL LIVE ON
by Geoff Larcom
Ann Arbor News, December 29, 2003

The Del Rio Bar is set to close this week.

With that, Ann Arbor will lose a little chunk of its character, a truly original and quirky joint founded in 1970 at the corner of Washington and Ashley Streets.

For me, it was the perfect downtown escape.

Behind that flickering red Del Rio neon sign and the shutters lay a quiet place where conversation and connection ruled, along with a little jazz music.

How many of you have had a Del Rio moment, a special one-on-one chat or gathering of friends that felt so intimate or comfortable that you remember it years later?

I always counted the Del as one of the four places I'd want to visit if I had to leave Ann Arbor in a week. . . .

Oh, sure, the Del Rio staff could be inattentive or self-absorbed at times. But most of them had interesting stories to tell, and it was one of the few places where you'd see the same people year after year. They weren't just college students passing through.

Contrast that with the many generic or more expensive places popping up, and it's worth taking a moment to embrace an old friend before it turns out the lights for good after New Year's Eve.

You'd enter and it would take a minute for your eyes to adjust. You'd see the tapes lining the bar and the glowing candles at each table.

If you were lucky you might even get served some food in a reasonable amount of time, including the signature Detburger: a high-class patty soaked in beer. (The burger was named after a former employee.)

But I didn't go in there to dine. I went in to enjoy somebody's company in a quiet hideout where you could really lose yourself.

Strolling around downtown and then walking in to the Del Rio after a University of Michigan hockey game with it snowing outside was to me the ultimate in old Ann Arbor comfort.

One of my Del Rio moments came when I met a longtime family friend there who had gone off to work for a paper in Vermont. He was a great conversationalist and he had stories to tell about covering a nuclear plant controversy.

I met him about 4 p.m. after work one bright spring afternoon nearly 20 years ago, and we talked and talked.

We lost track of time and our own concerns during one of those animated chats where the world shrinks to your table.

Hours later, I finally walked out into the evening sunlight, dazzled by the talk and disoriented, not from drinking but from the otherworldly feeling of the Del Rio.

You probably have your own Del Rio story, and it might not even be all happy. The place could rub some the wrong way.

But the Del also had an identity and a defining philosophy as the staff operated for many years as a cooperative. It had regulars and characters.

Now the Del Rio is losing money, and it's hard to tell who's at fault. It could be new management or the longtime staff or just the inevitable and wearing effects of time.

Ann Arbor changes, piece by piece. Some of the changes are good; some are bad. It's foolish to think the town would remain the same as it was when we grew up.

That would be pretty boring, wouldn't it?

But as I sit in a traffic jam next to one of those new eating places that you see advertised on TV, it becomes even more clear: There is only one Del Rio Bar.

Epilogue I

When Timothy Leary urged people to "turn on," it was not necessarily with drugs, he later explained, although drugs could act as a catalyst. For Leary, "turning on" meant to "Activate the divinity inside you, understand it and then create." Creating a new lifestyle and a better world was a goal among radical sixties youth who broke free from the tired ways and lies of their parent's generation.

Boomer's parents were shocked when their children went through those changes and they blamed it on drugs. "How can they take drugs?" cried the anguished, blameless adults who had been mired in their own drug world for years. They woke up with coffee, stayed awake with No-Doz, relaxed with booze or Valium and stopped the pain of their tense lives with Anacin or Bufferin. During the formative years of sixties youth, the media promoted a variety of cure-all drugs. Youth saw the power of the pill to alter physical states. Why not a little chemical theology to alter mental states, too?

Redefining themselves, sixties youth adopted styles of the past for tribal identification: the respect for Mother Earth of Native American culture combined with the principles of our founding fathers for a government that truly represented its people. They recoiled at the mess their parent's generation had created in Vietnam: "White men sending black men to kill yellow men to protect land stolen from red men."

Sixties youth set about shedding their parents' twisted values and hang-ups. They assumed the authority to create a new lifestyle in which to live their dreams. For that shining period of late sixties magic, no matter when it personally happened, those who fervently believed in it created a new world. For many of that era, the "sixties" was a fad and a fashion, but for those who lived it with all their heart, that fervor continues to shape their lives to this day. The seeds sown back then continue to slowly grow.

The sixties magic found a home at the Del Rio Bar in November of 1969 and it never left until the place closed in 2004. The original vision survived through constant clarification and the sometimes difficult implementation of changes. The Del Rio kept and nurtured what was best about the vision. New workers continued that vision as older workers moved on to other ventures or started families.

In the summer of 1995 a reunion of all who had ever worked at the Del Rio was held to celebrate the quarter-century mark. On the banks of the Huron River young, current workers joined old-timers and their children for a picnic and socializing. Lenny and his wife brought their teenage daughter—they had first brought her to the Del Rio when she was one week old (her parents had met there and had their wedding reception there, too).

Lenny asked one of the young workers what he thought of "us old farts." The young man looked Lenny over, shook his head and said, "Well, I know you worked at the Del Rio, so I figure you had to have been cool at one time." Lenny and his wife laughed at the divine retribution. The river kept flowing.

Jimi Hendrix was prescient when he sang:

"And if six turns out to be nine, I don't mind,
And if all the hippies cut off all their hair, I don't care."[49]

The nineties felt like the flip side of the sixties, but by then it was the children of Boomers who were rebelling against their parents. The new kids tired of hearing about the sixties, even as they exhibited similar values and styles of dress. They knew they could no longer shock their parents with long hair, so they dyed it green or shaved it or pierced parts of their face. They adopted silly styles while dismissing the sixties as being about silly styles. But similar values still lie beneath their gaudy exteriors, although they were less idealistic until 2008.

Sixties youth held many causes dear, but they rallied around one large effort: to end the war in Vietnam. Today we have another interminable, futile war in Iraq. Youth are getting killed in another far-off land, yet today's youth back home are strangely silent. Many feel powerless. Many more are distracted by the snares of consumerism—portable video games, cell phones, MP3 players, laptops—technology that did not exist in the sixties now occupies the time and money of modern children.

And these children have their own drugs of preference. Sure, pot is a timeless high and LSD is still available. But dangerous drugs have become more popular: crack, heroin, meth, ecstasy, even huffing aerosols. The failed war on drugs has been going on for decades and has done nothing to stop the flow, because it is based on simple supply and demand. The lure of massive profits on both sides of the law keep the status quo.

Despite some bad drug habits, today's youth are wiser about the world and their bodies. They distrust the government. Many are becoming vegetarians. They network with like-minded souls on the Internet. This gives aging boomers some solace, since efforts to "change the world" have taken so many years and there is still so much to be improved upon.

The presidential election of 2008 gave both liberal Boomers, and their jaded children renewed hope. They voted in unheard of numbers, along with the millions disgusted with the train wreck of George W. Bush's presidency. Their voices were heard as Barack Obama became the first black president, as well as the first post-Boomer president ever elected. Obama rekindled the hope and optimism of the sixties. During a period some have compared to the Great Depression, Obama offered a needed change, reminding us we are not the red states or the blue states; we are the United States.

Perhaps echoes of that old song rattle in Boomer brains: "Come on people now, smile on your brother, everybody get together and love one another right now." Or, as Wavy Gravy said, "It's never too late to have a happy childhood."

The original Del Rio generation is gray and wrinkled now, but they still carry bits of that old idealism that got them through their wilder days. They have retained the seeds of hope, slowly incubated them, and they now seem to be sprouting.

The revolution is not dead. It continues in the hearts and minds of those who lived through that magical time when all things were possible, when they were young and free and rocking to the beat of Peace, Love, and the Del Rio Bar.

Larry Behnke, former waitperson at the Del Rio Bar, current artist, photographer, writer and still a hippie.

Fission Fashion

> When nuclear dust has extinguished their betters,
> Will the turtles surviving wear people-neck sweaters?[50]

—Yip Harburg

Epilogue II

As Isaac Newton explained, with every reaction there is a counter reaction; historians called this the Thermidorean reaction, which described the dictatorship of Napoleon after the French Revolution. Thus back in the sixties the neoconservatives began their plan to destroy the "liberal" counterculture and create their own social ultraconservative takeover. They started with Nixon-Agnew et al., but by 1975 all had been indicted for various crimes; twenty-four of Nixon's men were jailed and Nixon was almost impeached but resigned in time to avoid jail. Congress abolished the House Un-American Activities Committee in the early seventies. But, never daunted, neocons elected Reagan—who tried to eliminate the Department of Education(!)—then Bush I, who lost to Clinton, but the movement reached its goals with Bush/Cheney in 2000. The Senate, House, and presidency went to one party that began moving toward a soft tyranny in American governance.

This radical right-wing regime, as noted in John Dean's *Conservatives Without Conscience*,[51] believed in neither equality nor democracy and were not, as Bush/Cheney asserted, either compassionate or conservative; they then tried to dismantle the Social Security program, labor unions, taxes for the rich, and so on. Their method was to rule with an authoritarian style by noblesse oblige, daily communion with the supernatural, and controlling the message by manipulating the national media. Their societal purposes, as these ideologues believed, were plutocracy, imperialism, and a whiff of theocracy. The Iraq War II became more disastrous than Vietnam. The war was not only a "fiasco," as Richard Ricks labeled it,[52] but it was deeply destructive of American ideals and conduct at home and in the world.

After six years of Bush/Cheney neocon extremism in the service of the right wing, by 2006 the American public had voted the ideologic and now corrupt Republican Party into a "robust minority" status in the U.S. House, Senate, and governorships as well as some state legislatures.

Secretary of Defense Rumsfeld, Cheney's man, was asked to resign. A promise of "bipartisan *consensus*" was made by Democratic Party leaders. Two African-Americans became chairs of Congressional Committees: one, the House Ways and Means Committee with oversight of tax policy, Social Security, and Medicare, and the other, the House Judiciary Committee. About forty-three African-Americans emerged in Congress, compared with thirteen in 1969. *The United States Senate was (is) still all white* except for Barack Obama, but he who embodied the progressive movement in American history began a new miracle in America by winning the highest office. By becoming its 44th president and its first black president, America is truly beginning on a path towards an equality dreamed of since 1776. Obama's major ability to cross all rival factions and create *consensus* on larger issues by compromises among all parties is an application of the democratic process to the national politic.[53] The first woman became Speaker of the House of Representatives, second in line to the presidency behind the vice president. There were more women in Congress in 2006—about 20 percent—than ever before in history! (Women were given the vote in 1920.) The first woman was almost elected president in 2008 (wait until next time!). The first openly gay representative became chair of the House Financial Services Committee. "The Times They Are a-Changin.'" The counterculture revolution of change in the sixties and seventies was at last bursting from the civil rights, women's rights, gender rights, antiwar, and antiauthoritarian movements that initiated them—all now in counterresponse to the Bush/Cheney radical right-wing governance. American democracy works its cyclic magic.

In Michigan, a woman Democratic governor, along with a woman senator, were reelected. Ann Arbor's City Council was solidly Democratic. A new electronic movement and private enterprise called Google moved into Ann Arbor with a radically new workplace environment.[54] Another year of "zero" homicides was recorded for the still 115,000 city of Ann Arbor, whose rare city charter restricts further land acquisitions.

The Del Rio Bar, however, was sold to the next-door Grizzly Peak Corporation, a nineties hard-line corporate yuppie bar-restaurant.

Now the country and people of the Del Rio Bar can move on and learn from the past about "executive *consensus*," legislative "multi-partisan *consensus*," and "multinational and diplomatic *consensus*," for example, North Korea, Northern Ireland. Obama will keep alive the permanent American vision of a democratic society. We must dare to alter radically the ancient political and social habits and thoughts of aristocratic leadership, acquisitive capitalist excesses, and military-industrial-congressional imperialism. The micro-experiment of a democratic workplace at the Del Rio Bar raises issues about that great American vision. Philosophical about the Del Rio's demise, "We had," Harburg says, "a hell of a run."

Ernie Harburg, former co-owner of the Del Rio Bar, Ann Arbor, Michigan, 1969-2004

"ONE SWEET MORNING"

Out of the fallen leaves
The autumn world over,
Out of the shattered rose
That will smile no more.

Out of the embers of blossoms
And ashes of clover,
Spring will bloom
One sweet morning.

Out of the fallen lads
The summer world over,
Out of their flags plowed under
A distant shore.

Out of the dreams in their bones
Buried under the clover,
Spring will bloom
One sweet morning.

One sweet morning
The rose will rise
To wake the heart,
And make it wise!

This is the cry of life
The winter world over,
Sing me no sad amen,
But a bright encore!

For out of the flags and the bones
Buried under the clover,
Spring will bloom . . .
Peace will come . . .
One sweet morning.[55] —Yip Harburg

"THAT GREAT COME-AND-GET-IT-DAY"

"On that great "come and get it" day,
Won't it be fun when worry is done
And money is hay?
That's the time things'll come your way,
On that great, great "Come and get it" day.

I'll get my gal that calico gown.
I'll get my mule that acre of groun'
'Cause word has come from Gabriel's horn
The earth beneath your plow is a-buddin'
And now it's your'n.

Glory time's comin' for to stay
On that great, great "Come and get it" day! . . .

Sez here!
Sez it in the good book, it sez
A mighty mornin' is nigh
Universal Fourth of July
Gonna get your freedom and pie!
Freedom, freedom, freedom, freedom pie!

What a day for banjos ringin',
What a day for people in overalls.
Can't you hear all the angels singin'?
Come and get your gravy and two meat balls . . . .

Bells will ring in every steeple
Come and get your test on the movie screen

Come you free and you equal people.

Come and get your beer and your benzedrine.

Sez here, come and get it, come!

There's gonna be a world shakin',
Bread breakin' day!

Great day! . . .

My gown will be a calico gown,
My feet will dance all over the town,
'Cause word has come from Gabriel's horn
The earth beneath your plow is a buddin'
And now it's your'n.

Glory time's
Comin' for to stay,
On that great, great
Come and get it,
And keep it,
And share it,
Great, great
Come and get it day![56]

—Yip Harburg

Some Notes About Consensus

The discovery of a group/collective process for making decisions affecting all group members probably derives from collective life among primates[57]. These decisions were of course non-verbal – a completely unknown, unresearched area of knowledge. Even among homosapiens, language-using executive groups in large-scale organizations not only suffer from "group think" but "non-think." Quaker religious groups operate on open-agenda, group consensus to make decisions. Among the six tribes or nations of the Iroquois Confederacy observers documented usage of consensus among chiefs and tribes with full authorship in the consensus process in which each and all tribal members participated, especially, most unlike Euro-American history, with full equality for women.[58]

In science also consensus reigns: The "paradigm shift"[59] is a consensus about strategy for research exploration. Furthermore, a so-called fact is a consensus of credibility given by fellow scientists to a hypothesis with a limited number of replications (some with negative results) to be replaced by future research findings. Finally, large laboratories working in various disciplines sponsor workshops on a selected topic for specialists across focused disciplines. "The idea behind such a gathering is that if the people who are world experts on the topic—often contentiously holding opposite views— can come to some sort of an agreement about certain aspects of the problem, science can move forward relatively more quickly.[60]

For industrial development, the concept is that the standards criteria are done through a consensus of industrial producers and users, government, academia, and end consumers, representing all sectors of the marketplace in which the standard is used and by all who could be impacted by the outcome of a standard. A voluntary consensus standard is developed by a cross section of stakeholders with an interest in the use of the product.[61] The time for such consensus varies from a few months to years.

Recently it has become almost requisite that criteria for creating the standards for planetary regulation of GlobalWarming can only logically be done through consensus of all nations in the United Nations.

The United States jury system is run on consensus.

The framers of the Constitution of the United States reached their agreements through consensus—often through creative compromises grudgingly agreed to by members who differed sharply on certain ideas. Specific wordings helped arrive at agreements. Unfortunately, the seeds of slavery were left in the document and many years later erupted and violence was unable to be contained. Even in the U.S. Senate, which was created for consensus as a major method of conflict resolution, violence erupted pre-Civil War. In the House of Representatives the practice of "bipartisan agreements," that is, consensus, was encouraged between the two-party antagonists. These agreements emerged from special committees designed to allow consensus processes to prevail, that is, voting gave way to group agreement. Finally, it must be noted that leadership in "facilitation," "compromise," "mediation," and soft enforcement of rules of courtesy are required for consensus to succeed.

One major dilemma of a democratic process is the problem of abuse of power by the majority. "The true or general will [of the people] is not invariably the same as the majority decision. . . . Madison's . . . hope was that the Constitution would make possible the conditions necessary to . . . a consensus made possible by repeated consideration of measures, one that would be more truly in the general interest than the result of a single, probably a hasty and inadequately considered, choice [by a simple majority]."[62]

In the world of musical theatre, collaboration and consensus is one of the key parts of "the creative process."[63]

Consensual decisions should hold, especially in families and in close-living relations such as cohabitation and marriage.

One of the several critical mechanisms (besides majority voting) of democratic governance is the process of consensus and much more scientific research should be devoted to the basic set of rules involved.

Science, secular morality, consensual conflict resolution, and secular government with the consent of the governed pro-tected by their human rights—not war, not the supernatu-ral, and not authoritarian ideologies—are the paths for the human race to develop a good society. May the long struggle move on!

—Ernest Harburg
—Observations by a Homo Sapien,
    American scientist and idealist in his
    eightieth year on the planet Earth

The history and legacy of the Del Rio is summed up brilliantly by Leigh Donaldson in the March-April 2018 issue of *Michigan History* magazine.[64]

Endnotes

1. Based on a quote by Albert Camus in *Bartlett's Familiar Quotations*, 16th ed. (Little, Brown, 1992), p. 732.

2. "All You Need Is Love" by John Lennon. ã 1967, Northern Songs. CD: *The Beatles: 1967–1970*. Capitol B000002UZ1.

3. "Over the Rainbow" by E.Y. Harburg and Harold Arlen. From *The Wizard of Oz*, 1939. ã 1939 (Renewed) EMI Feist Catalog, Inc. All Rights Reserved. Used by permission. Warners Bros. Publications US Inc., Miami FL 33014. CD: *Yip Sings Harburg*. Koch International KC7386.

4. "Ain't It de Truth?" by E.Y. Harburg and Harold Arlen. ã 1942 (Renewed) EMI Feist Catalog, Inc. All Rights Reserved. Used by permission. Warner Bros. Publications U.S. Inc., Miami FL 33014. CD: *Jamaica* original 1957 Broadway cast album. BMG-RCA 09026-68041-2 (1995).

5. Bernard Rosenberg, *Dictionary for the Disenchanted* (Chicago: Henry Regnery, 1972), p. 14.

6. Harburg and Arlen, "Ain't It de Truth?"

7. Adapted from Thucydides as quoted at www.worldofquotes.com/author/Thucydides/1/index.html.

8. Thomas Jefferson, letter to William S. Smith, 1787.

9. Adapted from Thomas Paine, *The Rights of Man* (Adamant Media Corp., 2000).

10. Erving Goffman, *Asylums* (New York: Doubleday Anchor, 1961), p. 305.

11. Abraham Lincoln, "The Gettysburg Address," November 19, 1863.

12. Barack Obama, Inaugural Address, January 20, 2009. http://obamaspeeches.com.

13. *The Lenny Bruce Originals*, Vol. 1 and 2. (Fantasy, 1992).

14. Kenneth Rexroth, *Bird in the Bush: Obvious Essays* (New York: New Directions, 1959).

15. Jack Kerouac, *On the Road* (Penguin Classics, 2002).

16. Robert Griffith, *The Politics of Fear: Joseph R. McCarthy and the Senate* (University of Massachusetts Press, 1987).

17. William H. Whyte and Joseph Nocera, *The Organization Man* (University of Pennsylvania Press, 2002).

18. E.Y. Harburg, *Rhymes for the Irreverent* (Madison, WI: Freedom from Religion Foundation, 2006; first published New York: Grossman, 1965; also reissued by The Yip Harburg Foundation, 1999).

19. *Essential Bob Dylan*. Sony B000050HTO.

20. Martin Meredith, *The Fate of Africa: From the Hope of Freedom to the Heart of Despair—A History of 50 Years of Independence* (Public Affairs, NewEd Edition, 2006).

21. Marylou and Jerome Bongiorno, *Revolution '67* (2007), documentary about the Newark uprising of July 1967; available at www.bongiorno-productions.com.

22. Nick Kotz, *Lyndon B. Johnson, Martin Luther King Jr. and the Laws That Changed America*, reprint (Mariner Books, 2006).

23. William H. Chafe, *Civilities and Civil Rights: Greensboro, North Carolina, and the Black Struggle for Freedom* (Oxford University Press, 1980); James W. Silver. *Mississippi: The Closed Society* (New York: Harcourt, Brace and World, 1963).

24. Scott Ainslie. *Blues Notes*, May 2007; available at http://blog.myspace.com/index.cfm?fuseaction=blog.view&friendID=128237062&blogID=264085177&MyToken=284ebf33-f6a7-4939-a746-d62c08382d97/.

25. Eric Alterman, *When Presidents Lie: A History of Official Deception and Its Consequences* (New York: Viking, 2004).

26. Alexis de Tocqueville, *Democracy in America* (Penguin Classics, 2003).

27. American Bar Association Legal Education Statistics, www.abanet.org/legaled/statistics/stats.html.

28. Linda Greenhouse, *Becoming Justice Blackmun: Harry Blackmun's Supreme Court Journey* (Times Books, 2005).

29. Catharine A. MacKinnon, *Are Women Human? And Other International Dialogues* (Cambridge, MA: Belknap Press of Harvard University Press, 2006).

30. Rick Goldsmith, director. *The Most Dangerous Man in America*. Kovno Communications, 2009.

31. *Bill Moyers Journal*, PBS TV, May 9, 2008.

32. Neil Gordon, *The Company You Keep* (Penguin Reprint Edition, 2004).

33. Amy Swerdlow, *Women Strike for Peace: Traditional Motherhood and Radical Politics in the 1960s* (University of Chicago Press, 1993).

34. E. Harburg, J.C. Erfurt, L.S. Hauenstein, C. Cape, W.J. Schull, and M.A. Schork, "Socioecological Stress, Suppressed Hostility, Skin Color and Black-White Male Blood Pressure: Detroit," *Psychosomatic Medicine* 35 (1973): 276. In *Toward an Integrated Medicine: Classics from Psychosomatic Medicine, 1959–1979* (Washington, DC/London: American Psychiatric Press, 1995).

35. E. Harburg, W.J. Schull, J.C. Erfurt, and M.A. Schork, "A Family Set Method for Estimating Heredity and Stress: I. A Pilot Survey of Blood Pressure Among Negroes in High and Low Stress Areas, Detroit, 1966–67," *Journal of Chronic Diseases* 23 (1970): 69.

36. Larry Behnke, "Peace, Love and the Del Rio Bar," unpublished typescript (1997). All extracts in this book, unless otherwise noted, are from this source.

37. Harold Meyerson and Ernie Harburg, *Who Put the Rainbow in The Wizard of Oz? Yip Harburg, Lyricist* (University of Michigan Press, 1995).

38. A documentary about Yip Harburg by Amy Goodman and her staff at *Democracy Now*, which combines Amy's 1996 interview of Ernie

Harburg with archival footage; available at www.democracynow.org/article.pl?sid=03/04/07/0234246.

39. Bret Eynon and the Contemporary History Project, eds. *Something Exploded in My Mind: Voices of the Ann Arbor Anti-War Movement—An Oral History Sampler* (Ann Arbor, MI: Contemporary History Project, 1981).

40. E.Y. Harburg, *Rhymes for the Irreverent*.

41. Ibid.

42. In Betty's words: "I added up the total number of hours worked in the bonus period. Then I divided the amount of money we were giving them (the total bonus) by the number of total hours worked. That gave a base amount for each hour. Using that number I multiplied that times the hours each employee worked, and that was the amount they received."

43. Jan Schlain, "Showdown at the Del Rio," *Ann Arbor Observer*, January 2004, p. 23

44. "The Party's Over," from *Bells Are Ringing* (1956), words by Betty Comden and Adolph Green, music by Jule Styne. ã 1956. Stratford Music Corporation c/o Chappell & Co., Inc. c/o Warner Chappell Music, Inc.

45. Sanford Levinson, *Our Undemocratic Constitution: Where the Constitution Goes Wrong (And How We the People Can Correct It)* (Oxford University Press, 2008).

46. Bernard Rosenberg, *The Province of Sociology: Freedom and Constraint* (New York: Crowell, 1972).

47. Ernest Harburg, "Research Map," *American Scientist* 54 (1966): 470.

48. Charles S. Peirce, *The Essential Peirce: Selected Philosophical Writings, 1867-1983*, ed. Nathan Houser and Christian J.W. Kloesel (Peirce Edition Project, 1992).

49. Jimi Hendrix ã 1967, MCA Records.

50. E.Y. Harburg, *Rhymes for the Irreverent*.

51. John Dean, *Conservatives Without Conscience* (Viking Adult, 2006).

52. Thomas E. Ricks, *Fiasco: The American Military Adventure in Iraq* (Penguin Press, 2006).

53. Jo Becker and Christopher Drew, "Pragmatic Politics, Forged on the South Side," *NY Times*, May 11, 2008.

54. Saul Hansell, "Google Answer to Filling Jobs Is an Algorithm," *New York Times*, Business Section, January 3, 2007.

55. "One Sweet Morning," words by E.Y. Harburg, music by Earl Robinson. ã 1971, Glocca Morra Music and Earl Robinson Music Exclusive Print Rights Administered by Hal Leonard Music Publishing Co., Inc. All Rights Reserved. Used by Permission. Performed by Ben Harburg on *Yip Harburg's Lyrics of Social* Comment (DVD, 2004; available from The Yip Harburg Foundation, www.yipharburg.com / e@ yipharburg.com).

56. "That Great Come-and-Get-It Day," from *Finian's Rainbow*, 1947. Music by Burton Lane. ã 1947, Warner-Chappell and Glocca Morra Music. Exclusive Print Rights Administered by Hal Leonard Music

Publishing Co., Inc. All Rights Reserved. Used by Permission. CDs: *Finian's Rainbow* original 1947 Broadway cast album, Sony B00004THLV (2000). Irish Repertory Theatre's 2004 Off-Broadway revival cast album, Ghostlight Records 184402 (2005).

57. *The Gorilla King*, David Allen, director. Segment of Public Broadcasting System's *Nature* series, 2008.

58. Sally Roesch Wagner. *Sisters in Spirit*. Native Voices Book Publishing Company, 2001.

59. Thomas S. Kuhn, *The Structure of Scientific Revolutions* (University of Chicago Press, 1962).

60. Daniel J. Levitin, *This Is Your Brain on Music: The Science of a Human Obsession* (Penguin, 2006), p. 172. Henry J. Stremba and Wayne P. Ellis, *Plain Talk: The Legacy of William T. Cavanaugh* (American Society for Testing and Materials, 1990).

61. *Handbook of Standardization: A Guide to Understanding Standards Development Today*, astm.org/cgibin/SoftCart.exe/NEWS/handbook 02/index.html?L+mystore+iail7686+1061332468.

62. Benjamin F. Wright, ed., *The Federalist* (Barnes and Noble, 1996), p. 84.

63. Bernard Rosenberg and Ernest Harburg. *The Broadway Musical: Collaboration in Commerce and Art*. NYU Press, 1993. See Part III.

64. Leigh Donaldson. "The Del Rio Bar: A Collective Human Resource Management Model That Lasted Thirty-Five Years." Michigan History, Mar.-Apr. 2018, pgs. 44-47.